A ROOM WITH A DARKER VIEW

A Room with
a Darker View

A ROOM WITH A DARKER VIEW

Claire Phillips

DoppelHouse Press | Los Angeles

A Room with a Darker View:
Chronicles of My Mother and Schizophrenia

Cover design: Nike Schroeder
Photograph by Mara Feder
Book design: Jonathan Yamakami

Publisher's Cataloging-in-Publication Data

Names: Phillips, Claire, 1965-, author.
Title: A room with a darker view : chronicles of my mother and schizophrenia / Claire Phillips.
Description: Los Angeles, CA: DoppelHouse Press, 2020.
Identifiers: LCCN: 2020936498 | ISBN: 9781733957908 (pbk.) | 9781733957984 (ebook)
Subjects: LCSH Phillips, Claire. | Schizophrenics--Family relationships--Biography. | Mother and child--Biography. | Mentally ill--Family relationships--Biography. | Schizophrenia--Treatment. | Schizophrenia--Relapse. | Psychiatric hospital Care--United States. | BISAC BIOGRAPHY & AUTOBIOGRAPHY / Personal Memoirs. | PSYCHOLOGY / Psychopathology / Schizophrenia.
Classification: LCC RC514 .P482 2020 | DDC 616.89/80092--dc23

 DoppelHouse Press | Los Angeles, California

"It has been said of dreams that they are a 'controlled psychosis,' or, put another way, a psychosis is a dream breaking through during waking hours."
— Philip K. Dick, VALIS

1

the small cramped dark

"And when at last you find someone to whom you feel you can pour out your soul, you stop in shock at the words you utter—they are so rusty, so ugly, so meaningless and feeble from being kept in the small cramped dark inside you so long."

—Sylvia Plath, *The Unabridged Journals of Sylvia Plath*

inside you

When the policeman arrived at the wrong house, fire extinguisher in hand, I immediately perked up. "5 Dorset Road is across the street," my friend's mother Mrs. Lochbaum declared. Registering that this uniformed man and the accompanying sirens of the fire truck in the distance were headed for my home, I skittered across the Lochbaum's sloping green lawn to get a glimpse of the action.

In no time a small crowd had gathered around the leafy property. There was no evidence of flames or smoke, or my mother, who had sequestered herself in her upstairs bedroom of the two-thousand-square-foot, neo-colonial tract home in Berkeley Heights, New Jersey, as she did most hot summer afternoons. Aroused by the energized crowd, at six years old I became determined to plant upon Jimmy English, a same-aged neighbor from up the street, a kiss. His unwillingness to be kissed only heightened my enthusiasm. As I chased the small boy with the close-cropped reddish-brown hair about the steep slope of our front yard, between the tall tangle of sinister looking oaks and elms, doing my utmost to catch up with him, I grew dizzy with pleasure and excitement.

Meanwhile inside the house, my mother, who had had her ear plugs in and was not easily roused, was busy explaining to the many uniformed men that she had only meant to keep the small saucepan on the stove for a short while, until the water had boiled, to make herself a cup of coffee. It was common for my mother to turn on the stove and leave the water boiling in a small saucepan, forgetting about it long enough for it to burn completely dry, leaving behind a chalky black residue, sometimes even warping the metal.

After the firemen left, despite having burned a section of the kitchen wall behind the yellow enamel stove, and despite not having recognized the sounds of alarm ringing throughout the half-mile development or having sensed the smell of smoke until the firemen had broken down the front door, my mother continued to boil water for her coffee in multiple small pots, ruining them on a continuous basis.

It was no surprise that she had almost burned the house down. Not for me or for the neighbors, nor for my physicist father.

1967–1968

I was two-and-a-half years old when I first recognized that something was wrong. We were living in Oxford, England at that time, when my brother was born. My father had just returned from observing cosmic background radiation at Teide Observatory in the Canary Islands when he took me to the hospital to see my mother. After parking his red Rover, we entered the double doors of the hospital, the ground outside still wet from a brief afternoon shower. Cheerfully swinging my favorite box of sweets that my father had bought for me, I skipped through the entrance and down a long corridor.

Upon entering her room, I found my mother tucked into a twin bed, a glass thermometer clasped firmly between her lips.

"Mommy, are you sick?" I asked.

"Yes," she guffawed loudly. "Yes, I am."

A mild alarm set in. Without meaning to, my mother had disclosed a carefully guarded family secret.

Moments later, our family's new addition was wheeled into the room. Swaddled in a blanket, velvety fists clenched in sleep, my pale newborn brother's thrumming presence served to break the discordant spell.

Six months later

I recall my mother cooing delightedly as my brother crawled about the kitchen floor in diapers and a snug white t-shirt.

"I was stung by a bee," I notified my parents, clutching at a tender pale forearm.

Outside, a large swarm of bees circled about our garbage cans in the narrow walkway between our house and the back yard. I had been afraid of these bees but persevered in my march, buoyed by the following parental pronouncement: "If you don't trouble them, they won't trouble you."

That afternoon, steeling myself as I passed by the intimidating swarm, the adage was proven false, and I was stung.

"No, you weren't," my mother said. "Now shut up and eat your lettuce."

"Daddy," I turned for what I hoped would be a sympathetic ear, "I was stung by a bee."

My parents' attention diverted then to my brother crawling along the floor in a patch of bright sunlight.

"Never mind, Claire," my father responded in a soft register. "Just eat your lettuce."

"If you knew how it worked, you would die."

Shortly after my brother was born, I began to have a recurring dream. I would first see a midsection of a brain, followed by an eerie pronouncement: "If you knew how it worked, you would die."

Years later, reading H. P. Lovecraft's celebrated story of cosmic fear, "The Call of Cthulhu," I encountered the same feeling of self-revulsion and dread from its opening lines: "The most merciful thing in the world, I think, is the inability of the human mind to correlate all its contents. We live on a placid island of ignorance in the midst of black seas of infinity, and it was not meant that we should voyage far."

September 30, 1968

After a five-day voyage on the Queen Elizabeth, the largest passenger ship in the world, our British family arrived in Newark, New Jersey; my father, a budding physicist and member of the "brain drain" of scientific and technologically trained minds leaving for America, would begin work at Bell Labs, the renowned research arm of AT&T, credited for breakthrough innovations such as the transistor, the laser, and the first communications satellite.

It was here, working with Nobel Prize-winning scientists on superconductivity and the detection of cosmic microwave background radiation, which provided spectacular proof of the Big Bang Theory, that my father co-invented a detector, a micron in size, which would launch the remainder of his career.

1968–1971

In New Jersey with time on her hands, determined to turn out her brood's first genius, my mother taught me to read. The time spent with my mother seated on her disheveled bed was grueling. I often stumbled over words beginning with or containing the digraph "th" and its preponderance of pronunciations as in the case of "this" or "breathe."

"We just had that word over here," she would snap, causing me much consternation.

I grew anxious during these drawn-out sessions and longed to be released from the gloom of my mother's heavily curtained room. Together we read the slim Ladybird pocket-sized books, purchased by my grandmother in England, featuring pale, carefully groomed Peter and Jane. Nonetheless I was a dutiful student, graduating quickly from one level of the keyword reading scheme books to the next. By the time I was in kindergarten, I had graduated to reading children's books: J. M. Barrie's *Peter Pan*, the series of *Wizard of Oz* books by L. Frank Baum, and *Mary Poppins* by P. L. Travers, among others. This was more a testament to my mother's indomitable spirit than to what she was sure was my inordinately high IQ.

When my brother learned to read, he was spared such brutal expectations. "Peter jumped into the pool," he cheerfully proclaimed, eyeing the pages of the open Ladybird book that sat perched between my mother's hands.

Pool? I peered in amazement. Peter, with his brown hair parted neatly on the side, was jumping from a tree branch into a natural body of water, a small stream or pond, but definitely not a swimming pool.

"There's not one letter in common between those two words," I cried foul.

The correct word was "water" but rather than berate my brother, my mother laughed with open delight.

On memory

At five years old, before falling to sleep, I would perform a slow review of the day's most salient moments, patiently waiting for them to register in vivid cinematic detail. The woods redolent with the fragrant smells of spring's first rain, or the terrifying moments, tightly ensconced within the folds of a scratchy blue blanket, precipitating my first altercation with my grandparents over a stolen box of candy.

The fastidious encoding of these episodic memories kept me preoccupied for long idle stretches alone in my room, the sun still bright in the early evening sky. That in short order these daily highlights would no longer assert themselves in rich sensory detail was a given. A slow degrade of these encoded scenes meant stories would become the inevitable next-best means for holding onto the past. Distinctly aware that I would not be able to rely on the instantaneous recall of my memory, I had to take extreme care to get the details right for these nightly performances. The stories were then safeguarded as the closest approximation to the truth that I might ever come to know.

Leaving for school each morning, the war between us intensified. *Remember to tell your teacher you can read,* my mother would scold me when she dropped me off at the top of Horseshoe Road, where a big yellow bus would show up like clockwork to usher us children three long blocks to the local public school. *Yes, Mummy,* I would respond dutifully, fully committed to doing just the opposite. (Our mother detested the Americanized *Mommy,* and forbade its use.) As the driver of the school bus lurched open the heavy metal door, my mother would then add the following caveat, *Remember to sit in the middle,* petrified that I might die or become severely injured in an accident on the short ride to Hamilton Elementary.

At home after school, I was then asked whether I had told my teacher I could read. "I forgot," was my usual excuse. I dreaded standing out among my peers. An immigrant with asocial parents, my predominant concern was to fit in. Finally my mother lost patience with my thin excuses and called the teacher, blowing my cover. To test my mother's claims, I was given *Bears on Wheels,* by Stan and Jan Berenstain. At first I thought my teacher was playing a practical joke on me. Why had she given me something this simple to read? Caution prevailed, and I did as I was told, assiduously reading the simple book out loud. In no time I was advanced to the first grade, where I soon learned that it was de rigueur to appear disinterested in whatever lesson was at hand. During reading group, our tall willowy teacher chalked the two-letter word "no" on the board.

"Now," she asked the group of students seated about the low school table, "can anyone tell me what this says?" No one raised a hand.

"Never tell anyone you are Jewish," my mother warned me. It was 1971. Nixon was in office advocating a New Federalism, and second-wave feminism had established itself with defiant protests and marches for equal opportunities and equal pay. Both my parents were of Jewish descent. For some reason, however, I was disallowed to speak of our heritage.

While my father enthusiastically toiled away at Bell Laboratories and my mother did her best to defy the conventions of housewifery, I played in the remodeled basement of Sally Gunning, a school friend who lived at the upper boundary of the Horseshoe Estates. Hers was one of five cookie-cutter homes in our small, two-mile square development, a hilly, exclusively white suburb of northeastern New Jersey.

Sally Gunning was the proud owner of a dizzying array of Barbies—a doll I was expressly forbidden from owning by my mother who deemed me too old at five for such claptrap. Reveling in the bending of Malibu Barbie's long, tapered appendages into a glut of modish poses, I was suddenly asked a revealing question.

"What religion are you?" Sally asked, blonde and superior in her fashionable plaid jumper. My mother's prohibitions on discussing the subject had not included an appropriate dodge. Unprepared, I stared blinkingly up at Sally.

"Christian," I managed to say after a decidedly awkward moment.

"Really?" she seemed excited. "What denomination?"

I searched blindly for an answer. Having never stepped inside a church or synagogue, I had precious little to offer on this topic. Finally I managed to issue forth a multi-syllabic answer, one that escapes me to this day.

"Wow," Sally enthused. "Me too!"

After this, I vowed never again to follow my mother's incomprehensible rules.

Horseshoe Estates Development

Everyone knew where the other three Jewish families in our subdivision lived. These homes were notably cared for better than ours, with their custom paint jobs, superior roofing, carefully clipped hedges, and shiny new cars parked out front. My parents were bookish, busy with invisible realities. Our cars were bought used and often in need of a paint job. The grass often went uncut in summer. Our back yard was flinty and covered in crab grass. And in the front, instead of the deliberately planted trees like the neighbor's, a copse of irregularly spaced mature elms and oaks loomed over our home like a sinister cabal.

The solicitous phone call we received each summer from a paint contractor came as no surprise. My father would confide to my mother in an aggrieved tone, "A neighbor has complained about us again. We are bringing down the neighborhood real estate values."

My mother's throaty laughter, a giddy pleasure in defying convention, would then be accompanied by my father's ironic grimace. In their derision of the neighbors, my parents were in complete accord.

Prejudice in our neighborhood was not restricted to religion. When the first African-American family purchased a house on Springfield Road, it was literally the talk of the town.

The prejudice grew even more apparent in fourth grade when my family migrated back to England for what turned out to be a brief time. In our absence, our home was rented to an African-American family, a fact never openly discussed in my household, perhaps because it was simply of no concern.

This move that would allow my mother to revive a hastily abandoned law career would not end well. In the summer of 1975, we emigrated back to the United States. While visiting a neighbor whose daughter I often babysat, I came to learn that our tenants had not been white.

"Did you have to fumigate your house?" our neighbor mockingly asked, supine on her redwood deck under the shade of a massive oak, the racial-hatred underpinning our white suburb erupting shockingly into plain view.

Don't!

Before my mother found purpose again, and whenever my father went out of town on business, I would be required to take his place in bed. *I'm afraid to be alone,* she would complain of her husband's lengthy absences. During those long, anguished nights I would lay on the hard mattress next to my mother, stricken. If I so much as moved a muscle, turned over or breathed too loudly, I would be sharply rebuked. *Stop moving.* Or, *Don't!* she would exhort in a threatening tone.

Too afraid to sleep, I would lie awake throughout the night, mesmerized by the steady rhythm of a popping sound—a bubble of spit that would form between my mother's lips and pop before another would promptly take its place. Mortified by this involuntary behavior of hers, I would bide my time waiting until she would turn over before I might attempt a stealth move. The heavy curtains of her bedroom drawn tight, I would wait until dawn for a chink of light to appear under a wide crack in the flimsy particleboard door to her bedroom. *May I go to my own room now, Mummy? Okay, darling,* she might murmur in her sleep.

Permission granted, I would traipse down the hallway to my bedroom, aggrieved and full of spite, vowing to grow up to be nothing like her. A foolish if spirited proposition.

Mrs. Dee's

My mother was a distant presence at best. Still she was a dutiful parent, enrolling us in summer classes like swimming and arts and crafts. Each summer I would take lessons at Mrs. Dee's Swim Club. The bathing suit I wore, a one-piece sailor's suit with its white pleated skirt, navy-blue bodice and bright red belt, excited me to no end. I loved any excuse to put it on and strut about the house during the hot months instead of wearing the obligatory frowsy dress.

I was not a good swimmer. In fact, I was lamentably bad. Deluded about my talents, at the end of each summer I would wait for the swim club bathing suit patch to arrive, commemorating that year's achievement. This was always anti-climatic. Before even opening the transparent waxy envelope, I would make the unhappy discovery that I never seemed to advance. The stitched image of a bathing-capped beauty diving into water that arrived in the mail was always a beginner's patch.

One afternoon I recall waiting for Mummy after swim class, the air strongly scented with chlorine. The last parent to arrive, a blur of pink lipstick and glossy dark hair, she appeared through the sunlit aperture of the doorway, a striking silhouette.

"Come on!" she commanded loudly in her accented, high-pitched voice. Her tone was distant. Disembodied. I understood that she was different from the other mothers. Though I could not have understood why.

The classics

Beyond early schooling, our mother didn't interact with us much. She may have simply found us children poor company. She was always so eager to get us to sleep. Most nights, even during those sun-filled summer evenings, we were squirreled off to bed, often as early as 5 p.m. We were also required to take two-hour naps during the day. To a young active child, this felt punitive. Anti-social. Foreboding.

Often my mother implored me to read "the classics." These were her childhood books that she kept for me on the top shelf of my spare closet. While she had perhaps intended that these musty, hard-backed keepsakes would be a sentimental gift, they symbolized for me a senseless captivity. My room, painted a gender-specific pink, was almost entirely bare. These books were its chief adornment, and for some time they were anathema to me.

One late afternoon, bored of empty midday hours spent alone in my room, I maneuvered a small wooden chair inside the closet to procure a book from the shelf. To my surprise, I discovered my mother's books were magical, rich and engrossing, not the turgid, joyless tomes I had feared. These were mostly late nineteenth-century and early twentieth-century fairy tales, coming-of-age tales, or adventures, the standard fare of mid-century children's literature: *Little Women*, *The Life and Adventures of Robinson Crusoe*, *The Three Musketeers*, *Little Lord Fauntleroy*, *The Secret Garden*.

While I lost myself in books, my mother was transported by internal rhythms of her own. Naked in a see-through pink nylon negligee and strappy heels, my mother swung her firm alabaster legs high in the air as she traversed the many rooms of our open-plan house, enraptured, humming and snapping her fingers in a clumsy syncopation.

Knowing something was wrong in our household, I chalked up most problems to my mother's poor character. She often attacked me for small infractions of household rules. And she held my father to similar impossible standards. My parents fought a lot in those days. I remember listening to her accusations after they returned home from parties, work parties usually. These arguments lasted long into the night. *I wasn't flirting with her. — You were. — I wasn't. — I saw you.* My mother wouldn't let up, and the misery of her relentless recriminations countered by my father's soft-voiced pleas was interminable.

After a time, I wanted my father to leave my mother, to go, maybe to an expensive hotel and recover his dignity. I believed she was in the wrong, and he the put-upon victim. My father was mild mannered, generally, and didn't have the time or the inclination to harangue his spouse. My mother harangued us all, often.

A year or so into these wearying bedroom wars, my father started threatening to leave. Late into the night he would make a show of packing his bags. My brother and I would marshal our forces, seizing his packed bag from the landing of the second floor of our home, squirreling his things back into the spare room as a strong declaration of love for him and some sort of misguided hope for our family unit. His case hidden, Dad would have no means of escape. As the fighting continued I grew more and more unsettled. It was demoralizing, and I felt embarrassed for him. Finally I had had enough and no longer orchestrated the hiding of his suitcase (my attempt at reconfiguring the domestic argument into a family hoot — *Where did you hide it? Ha, ha.*) During one of the last pretenses at separation, my father peered up at me from the bottom of the stairs, brown suitcase beside him on the black tile of the foyer, packed and ready to go.

"I won't go, Claire, if you don't want me to." My father's bright blue eyes bored into mine, pained and almost pleading.

This wasn't the outcome I had envisioned. I wanted my mother proven wrong. She couldn't harass us this way. But instead, I was being asked to thread together a family I naively wanted dissolved. In a willed tone of girlish need, I enacted for my father the words he wanted to hear: "Don't go, Daddy." And the suitcase was promptly put away.

Point Pleasant Beach

My father and I were born on the same day—April 18. Despite our similarities in some characteristics, we did not share the same proclivity for long, unrestrained conversation. From as young as five, I remember badgering my father on outings for answers on all conceivable topics. *But why Daddy? Why? Why?* Ignoring my ceaseless inquiries, he would drive on in silence. Later on, I tried engaging my father in passionate review of football, a sport he routinely tuned into on weekends, positioned a few feet in front of the black-and-white television in a velour, swivel bucket chair.

Daddy, I would ask, hoping to cheer on a favorite team, *Which team to do you want to win? The black team or the white team?* Sharing in an emotional identification with my father was a vain hope. *It doesn't matter*, he would answer in a barely detectable English accent, long legs neatly stretched out before him, eyes nearly closed.

In the summers, he often took us children to the Jersey

Shore, the scent of which I readily confused with that of the oil refineries along the Jersey Turnpike. The window of our vehicle cracked open, I would inhale deeply the acrid smell, almost swooning. *Ah, the beach*! I would exclaim giddily, my father always quick to correct me.

The mile-long Point Pleasant Beach, with its kid-friendly boardwalk and dynamic waves, was where we would play Skee-Ball, buy delicious clouds of cotton candy, and duck and dive under the waves close to the shore. When it was our father's turn to exercise, I would sit hunched on my towel and watch him swim out far beyond the waves in his light blue swim trunks, pale arms slicing through the Atlantic until he faded from view. A half-hour later Dad would return dripping wet to relax on his worn, brightly-colored towel. Stealthily I would observe the distinctive scar that ran the length of my father's lean torso, the result of a severe burn that he had incurred at eight years old when his younger brother tipped him in his chair too close to the fire. A mesmerizing scar that licked at his ribs like the dazzling rays of the sun.

Alter ego

During this time, my terahertz-wave pioneering father was almost always at "the labs," a term I confused readily with another oft-used term, "the lav;" an English colloquialism for the bathroom, someone in our household could be going to either *the labs* or *the lav*.

Joy, I'm leaving now for the labs. I won't be back until late. The close association of these terms disturbed me. Did my father work in a large porcelain toilet bowl?

In the high-ceilinged corporate brick building, my father participated in open discussions with Nobel laureates that led him to the invention of a radio receiver able to detect elusive elements in the interstellar medium. While my father's ambitions for success were being met at every turn, my mother's boredom and frustration was acted out upon her school-aged children. Like my father, she too had been educated at Oxford, yet her career aspirations remained unfulfilled.

Sometimes at night when I was meant to be in bed reading the Brother's Grimm or books by P. L. Travers, I would sneak downstairs to snatch glimpses of prime time television, and the myriad performers who entertained my father when he took those short breaks between long ten- and twelve-hour stints at Bell Labs. I was transfixed by one popular singer dressed in bell bottom pants and a button-down shirt of monochrome black who clasped a shiny silver bulbous microphone and belted out the lyrics of his latest hit song: *What's new, Pussycat? Woah, woah, woah.*

In the reflective glare of the family's small black-and-white television, I had discovered an alternate reality. This full-throated baritone with the coiffed head of dark curls was none other than my father. My reserved English father had ditched his commoner threads, the Marks and Spencer brand polyester pants and shirt sent to him all the way across the Atlantic Ocean by his mother, for the glamorous attire of the world renowned Welsh stage singer, Tom Jones. This was my father's alter ego. The two men even shared the same first name. This electrifying sight confirmed for me an unspoken truth—when my father was away from home, he led a glittering life, hips gyrating to the delight of a predominantly female audience.

The other Toms

There was a third Tom, or to be perfectly chronological, a second Tom. This second Tom sat at a desk in our dusty two-car garage selling homes in our subdivision. We were the first homeowners on the block, and my mother was very proud of this fact, citing it often. She was equally proud of an acquisition that set our property apart, the extra eighth of an acre of land. This forested, wild bit of earth, with its dense and overgrown blackberry bushes and dozens of mature trees separating our home from our neighbors was my mother's pride and joy.

During the warm summer months of our first year living in Berkeley Heights, my mother would often make her way from the kitchen into the laundry room in a colorful shift, raven-colored hair styled in the same flipped fashion as Marlo Thomas in *That Girl*, to present the handsome outsider ensconced in our garage with an icy can of Coca-Cola. As the mild flirtation flourished between housewife and contractor, I sensed in my mother something buoyant, almost delighted.

In this dream, I am in my father's large sedan. I am in the backseat, and he is in the driver's seat. The car is in motion when suddenly my father thrusts open his door and climbs out of the car. I panic, unsure which pedal is the brake and which is the gas. I am six or seven years old when I start having this dream.

For some reason, no matter how often I rehearse the mechanical knowledge of driving a car when I am awake, I am never able to translate this to my dream. Night after night, I am abandoned in a car that I cannot control.

Queen's Gate

Moving to New Jersey was not my mother's first migration, but her second. At eleven years old, her parents had sent her from Rhodesia to Queen's Gate, an elite all-girls boarding school nine thousand miles away in England, notably attended by the Redgrave sisters. Soon after, her two younger sisters followed. Because of the prohibitive expense of traveling back and forth between England and southern Africa, my mother rarely returned home, spending the better part of holidays with family in the U.K.

Over the years, I grew to think of my mother and her sisters as belonging to a strange cabal. Their mere existence suggested something vaguely troubling concealed beneath the suburban reality to which they aspired. They looked alike, with broad faces and distinctly shaped noses. Spoke in accents unlike anyone else's I knew. This southern African accent embodies an incomparably violent history. Influenced by years of English and Dutch settling and plundering of this Bantu-speaking region of Africa, it is a non-rhotic accent, one in which the phonemes, depending upon their placement, are not always pronounced.[1] For example "r" consonants are not always pronounced. The "r" of *hark* becomes "ha:k", and the "r" of *car* becomes "ca:" My name pronounced by my mother sounded something like "cla:."

Sharing a common destiny, one by one after college, these three women immigrated to America so their husbands could find jobs and they could start families. Staying close to each other was not the determining factor. The impetus was economic. My mother's youngest sister moved to Staten Island with her husband, a Zionist and a doctor, who passionately taught his three children Hebrew in their refurbished basement. The middle sister moved to Houston and then Dallas with her French husband, also a doctor. My mother had been the first to arrive in the U.S., settling in New Jersey. Growing up, I felt certain that she, as the eldest, held the key to this family's destiny. Perhaps she did. But it was not the one I imagined.

---

1 Demirezen, Mehmet. "Which/r/Are You Using as an English Teacher? Rhotic or Non-Rhotic?" *Egyptian Journal of Medical Human Genetics*, 1 Sept. 2012. Web.

Of the three sisters, my Aunt Anne was considered to be the prettiest. From the warm tone of my father's voice, whenever he spoke of her I knew that he liked her best, maybe even more than his wife. Once, after visiting Anne and her family in Texas while on business, he told me that I looked like her. At six years old, I took this to be a compliment and also a terrible omen. I had just learned that my aunt had lost one of her legs in a car door. This triggered in me great confusion. I would speculate on possible scenarios while seated in the back of my parents's station wagon, wondering why no one had come to my aunt's aid. I became mordantly afraid of this vehicle with its outlandish powers. How was it even possible to lose a leg through the simple closing of a car door? You couldn't possibly do that to yourself, could you? And if someone else were to close the door on your leg, surely this someone would hear you scream out for help. It was bewildering to say the least.

Years later, I heard stories from other relatives about how my aunt had lost her leg. The first story was that at eighteen years old she had fallen in love with a Christian boy. Grandpa Mike, a reverent Jew, prohibited the relationship. In despair, she swallowed an entire bottle of aspirin and hid inside a boudoir, inadvertently falling asleep for over twenty-four hours, cutting off the circulation to one of her legs. Years later, I was told by other cousins that after being denied the opportunity to leave southern Africa for college in England, she had threatened to commit suicide. When her parents left for a two-day research trip, she attempted to make good on her promise and consumed the bottle of aspirin.

Not all was discord. I remember those first years living on Dorset Road when our mother seemed almost content.

There was a neighbor my mother was willing to spend time with, Betty, who lived in a two-story Colonial at the end of our cul-de-sac and had three children, all boys with whom I loved to play. Her oldest son, Johnny, was a troublemaker of the first order and my idol, routinely chastised for his bad boy hijinks like smashing the neighbor's garage windows with rocks. Once while playing in the half-built foundation of a neighboring construction site, he smashed his brother Bobby's hand with a brick, nearly severing his three-year-old brother's pinkie finger from his hand.

That unforgettable spring afternoon, my mother was enlisted to drive Betty and her brood to the emergency room. No one cried, no one carped. A glorious drive then ensued with everyone piled into our sky-blue Ford station wagon, Betty and Bobby in the front seat, his partially severed finger wed delicately to his hand with a small hand towel, Johnny and the middle brother squeezed in back with my brother and me. I remembered being proud of my mother for doing her part without the fussing or tension that minor problems typically presented. However, this sociability and relative calm was not to last.

2

the creeping

in the patterns

A deferred career

In 1972, when the Equal Rights Amendment passed the U.S. Senate 84–8 and appeared on its way to being ratified, my mother became insistent that our family return to England, after living in New Jersey for just over five years, so that she could pursue a deferred career in law.

My mother liked to boast that my father would never have taken the research position at Bell Labs without her prompting. This job that would launch a rewarding career and a twenty-five year professorship at CalTech, where he observed suborbital space in NASA airplanes and directed one of the world's first sub-millimeter telescopes; this job, which culminated in working with the European Space Agency to send experimental equipment into deep space to detect dark matter, would have been unwittingly passed over by my father if it were not for my mother's preternatural wisdom and clear-eyed practicality.

Summer 1972

He must have guessed something would be irrevocably lost. That summer our father acted to change the dynamic. Out of the blue he turned up one afternoon to arts and crafts, the summer program in which our mother had enrolled us. He was seated in his green Oldsmobile Cutlass Supreme, disconcertingly dwarfed behind the steering wheel of its long front end.

"Get in," he called out the window.

He was there to take us on an impromptu family vacation. This was a first—encountering our father in the middle of the day. Aside from trips to the beach on weekends or occasional visits to England, we rarely traveled. That night our family left by car for Montreal, a weekend trip that was destined to end almost as soon as it began. A minor disaster from the get-go, we spent half the night driving up and down the same unfamiliar stretch of highway, continually missing the off-ramp for our hotel, until my five-year-old brother pointed it out to my beleaguered father.

The hotel room was a prescription for terror. Located on the tenth floor of a newly erected skyscraper with mesmerizing floor-to-ceiling windows, I could not make my way beyond the midpoint of the room due to an extreme fear of heights. The following morning at breakfast before we had even begun our sightseeing, my mother declared her need to study. We had to return home, then and there. My father looked crushed, any hope of familial normalcy completely dashed.

Statistical anomaly

For the remainder of that summer, with formidable discipline, my mother studied for the British bar, barricading herself inside her bedroom, going so far as to lock my brother and me out of the house during the height of the hot, humid season. After a couple of hours of play, desperate for the comfort of central air conditioning, we would return home to find the front door locked. Resolute in her efforts to study, aided by pale pink wax and cotton earplugs worn throughout the day, she ignored our loud banging at the door, the ringing of the dual-tone door bell, until she had accomplished her goals.

One afternoon, irked by the sound of us playing inside, she complained to our father in loud accented bursts.

"They make so much noise. How can I study?"

After this outburst, I watched my father stand before the long bank of wide multi-paned windows, gazing distantly into our shady front yard, hands wadded in the pockets of his slim-line pants. He looked visibly trapped behind the glass, peering out onto our uncared-for front lawn, a single tear sliding down his cheek. It was the one time I would see my father cry. My mother left that September for England to sit for the bar. She passed on her first try. This seemed extraordinary, given the long break between school and her studies.

Why had my mother chosen to abandon her career in law in the first place? Did she suspect that she stood little chance to succeed? In that era, few women who passed the bar qualified for the position of solicitor and even fewer as a barrister. According to *BBC News*, in 1957 when my mother was studying for her A Level examinations at Oxford, only 1.94% of women completing the tests qualified as solicitors. In 1967, the number was 2.7%. In 1977, the number jumped to a mere 7.33%.[2]

2 "UK | 75 Years of Women Solicitors." *BBC News*, BBC, 19 Dec. 1997. Web.

Giving in

After passing the bar, my mother began to insist that my
father give up his work on superconductivity at Bell Labs
and that we move back to England so she could find work
as a barrister in criminal law at a chambers in London.
The only time I saw them touch was when she succeeded
in wearing him down after many months of determined
argument. When he finally agreed to move back, she threw
herself into his lap, triumphant. There my father sat under
my mother in his customary swivel chair where he dozed
between long stints at work, now with an odd grimace on
his face, arms languishing about the bucket-shaped sides
with my cheerful mother in his lap. For months, I had
begged my father to give in to her pleas to move back to
England. *You know you're going to do it, Dad. Just give in.*
The look on his face told me he was in some way pleased to
give her what she wanted.

My mother got her wish, and we moved back to England
at the start of what would have been fourth grade for me,
and what would have been first grade for my brother. My
father found employment as a reader in physics at London
University while he continued to work full time at Bell Labs.

Later when I asked him how this was possible, traveling
between two countries to work, he said he could only do it,
"because the students at the London University weren't much
good."

Watford, Hertfordshire

At first we stayed in Watford, an industrial town in the borough of Hertfordshire, seventeen miles northwest of London with my father's parents, in a large brick Edwardian house that had been converted into a boarding house. Life with my father's parents was fairly uncomplicated and by extension almost magical. The large house on Langley Road, walking distance from the Watford High Street Station, was bordered by beds of scented roses and lavender bushes, and shaded with magnificently tall and leafy chestnut trees. Behind the house was a long descending garden of manicured beds of flowers, massive hydrangea bushes and impossibly neat, clipped grass tended to weekly by my grandfather with his mid-century push-powered lawn mower. A twenty-foot rhododendron tree that grew wide and heavy with its massive pink, bell-shaped clusters of showy flowers and drapery of glossy green leaves provided a sanctuary in mid-summer. In this garden during World War II air raids, my father had hidden in a bomb shelter, been tormented by his younger brother of six years, and played with his model airplanes while hanging from the knobby limbs of massive chestnut trees.

In the dappled sunshine, I helped my grandmother hang the laundry outside and spent hours tossing an American football about with my grandfather, whose hopes for a college education had been dashed when his father died and he was required to take over the management of the family pub. Instead of becoming a writer as he had once dreamed, he worked as a traveling shirt salesman for most of his adult life, until he was finally able to obtain clerical work in a solicitor's office in his seventies.

On this tidy green lawn, my mother once performed several

immaculate cartwheels in a row, countering my father's disbelief in her ability to do so. This would be the only time I would witness my mother engaged in an act of play.

"See," she boasted to us children. "Your father says I can't do cartwheels, but I can."

1956–1974

In England, instead of eating meals comprised of cheap conveniences like frozen diced vegetables and flank steak, we delighted in fresh meats and fish purchased from the local butcher and markets, with their abundant foreign aromas. When my mother was out looking for a home or working at a London barrister's office, Granny Iris would take me into her confidence, telling me stories about my father, her firstborn and precious Tommy. My father was the first to attend college in his largely Ashkenazi Jewish family, whose lineage in England spanned the course of two centuries. In 1956, while studying physics at Oxford on a scholarship, he met my mother who was attending St. Anne's College, studying law.

As my grandmother told it, my parents met at a Jewish club on campus.

"Upon first sight, your mother made a beeline for your father," she confided. "She was ready to take him by storm." Apparently, my father was the gleaming trophy and my mother, the uncouth but lucky contestant.

I began to wonder if there had not been another more suitable woman out there, someone more pliable and less arrogant who might have won my father's affections had my mother not been, in my grandmother's estimation, so aggressive. Prior to the war, Jewish students generally chose to hide their religious background and ethnicity. Prejudice in England against Jews had been a long-standing practice. According to the Oxford Chabad society, the aftermath of World War II did much to change public perception of Jews:

> The war changed much in Oxford. Apart from a massive, though temporarily swelling of the Jewish population of Oxford, and the arrival of exotic European refugees, including Einstein, the war shattered the already tattered remnants of the social fabric of the old order in the Oxford colleges. Thus the postwar era saw a great expansion in the numbers of Jewish students attending Oxford, and an exceptional growth in the numbers of Jewish academics.[3]

I was surprised to learn that my parents had participated in any kind of social club. In their married life, they had little time for such frivolity.

---

3 Roberts, Marcus. "A Brief History of Jews of Oxford." *Oxford Chabad Society—Serving Oxford Jewish Students*, 2005. Web.

Summer 1960

The story of my mother and father's honeymoon goes something like this: Traveling one night in Germany, my father found himself driving the wrong way down a poorly lit, one-way road. Suddenly, a big rig appeared out of nowhere. My father managed to swiftly maneuver his small English car into a tight parking spot, failing however to position the car entirely out of harm's way. The truck clipped the rear end of his car, and my father was flung headlong into the windshield.

Not wearing his seat belt, my twenty-three-year-old father cracked his skull open. Meanwhile my mother, who was belted in, incurred minimal injuries—a light concussion and chipped front tooth. An augur of trouble to come.

1970–1973

In America, with my professionally educated English parents, I was markedly different from my peers, and often on the receiving end of thoughtless invective. Here, where my father grew up, I had hoped to find some sort of easy acceptance. This would not be the case. On the playground of my private school (what we call a public school in the U.S.), I was branded a "Yankee" and teased unmercifully until I finally adopted a British accent.

After that, I soon found my place at school. This would be a pivotal time, when I would discover I had some aptitude for writing. That term, our teacher arranged on a tall bookcase as many disparate yellow objects as she could find. We were required to choose one object as impetus for writing. I chose a vinyl purse and wrote about its mysterious contents: a matchbox containing an entire community of miniature people and witches, whose calibrated magic spells adhered to the powers of a waxing and waning moon. The story seemed to write itself—a reflection of the vast reading of children's literature I had done at my mother's direction.

My teacher deemed this an excellent story, and typed it up, before arranging for me to meet our headmaster. Intended as encouragement, this meeting was anything but inspirational. Seated before this figure of dispiriting authority, I was met with stony British derision.

"Now tell me," the tense-looking man interrogated, "which do you say? Cookie or biscuit?"

"Biscuit," I answered dutifully. Once again, I was being schooled in proper English. The lesson was a never-ending one.

At home things were no better. Apparently I had made a big mistake adopting the accent of my peers, I was soon to learn. *Why can't you speak like your mother?* my father would fume. *You sound like you grew up in the gutter.* I had no idea that the working class accent I had adopted would cause such a ruckus. Of course, what my father wanted from me was impossible. My mother had a southern African accent. While she had been schooled in England from the age of twelve, she had apparently not chosen to assimilate like I did. She had retained her accent with its high degree of German inflection. This distinguished her as someone who had grown up in a British colony, an outsider, and certainly not a member of the upper class. I could not discern the benefits of adopting her accent. With little understanding of English class structure, I could not yet pinpoint the intensity of my father's rancor.

Loughton, Essex

Our parents were rarely home. Our father was often traveling for work and our mother spent her time commuting to London to work in chambers.

It wasn't long before my mother purchased us a modest townhouse in Loughton, Essex. This northeastern suburb of London located on the edge of Epping Forest, known as "The People's Forest," the ancient woodland distinctive for its massive pollarded trees, is located at the end of the Central Line of the London Underground.

During this year-and-a-half while our mother was working, we had a number of babysitters and two live-in nannies from whom I learned firsthand of England's rigid class structure—one in which young girls who did not have the good fortune or opportunity to pass the 11-plus exam in school would go to work as live-in nannies for affluent families when they were sometimes as young as sixteen years old. I was especially enamored of our first nanny, Avril, who came to live with us at seventeen years old. Her father, I learned, had been a factory worker and was missing a finger. For my birthday, she bought me small gifts of a diary and a hairbrush, gendered frivolities I cherished. We counted on each other in small ways, and it was the first time I felt I could languish in the warmth of an adult who was not a family member. It felt exceptionally luxurious. My mother, however, did not seem to appreciate the help of this young woman.

Before giving her notice, one night Avril confided in me the distress she felt working for us.

"I can't keep cleaning up after your mother. Whenever I clean a countertop, she immediately spills coffee all over it. She is always making a mess. I just can't do it anymore."

There were other complaints about my mother and her perplexing obliviousness, but these did not seem to influence her behavior. Avril's departure was disappointing—our next nanny, Gail, was even younger still and not nearly as warm or steadfast. After six months, she too disappeared but not before playing for me The Who's rock opera album *Tommy* on her gramophone. *This part is for you,* she would say at the critical moment in "Smash the Mirror" when Tommy breaks through his psychosomatic illness. The sound of breaking glass would course loudly through her small bedroom. Her dedication left me feeling strangely humiliated and betrayed. What about my behavior had elicited this reaction?

Michael and Esther Gelfand

During gaps in childcare, my mother's parents took turns looking after us. First Granny Esther came to stay—an engaging, somewhat high-strung woman whose life was devoted almost exclusively to the care of her distinguished husband, Mike, and his all-encompassing career.

Granny provided us with the structured care we so sorely lacked. She would greet us at home after school in a kempt straight skirt, her bluish gray hair wound in a tight bun, with the "tea" she would set for us on the polished wood dining table: a glass of watered down orange squash, sections of peeled tangerines with a small bowl of peanuts and raisins. An effective homemaker, she would tell us fairy tales and help keep the house tidy. With our grandmother in residence, afternoons were mostly calm and cheerful. Only when she felt we weren't following one of our mother's tedious rules, would the peace be broken. She would grow hysterical, cry and barricade herself in her room, yelping in that signature high-pitched voice of hers that our mother was now going to be very cross with her because of our disobedience. I could not fathom how my grandmother allowed her daughter's temper to become the barometer of her actions. But there was not much I could do to win her over. Granny Esther's tears were simply too much to bear.

Soon after her departure, my highly accomplished and exceptionally driven grandfather would arrive. My mother's father, Michael Gelfand, the son of Lithuanian parents who had fled the violent anti-Semitic pogroms of the Russian Empire for South Africa at the turn of the twentieth century, had attended the University of Capetown to become a distinguished doctor and author. His expertise in researching subtropical diseases earned him an OBE and a Papal Order of the Knighthood of St. Sylvester. Founding professor of African medicine at the then-University of Rhodesia, there were few other doctors in then-Salisbury—or, for that matter, the rest of the country—with my grandfather's stature. In his lifetime he wrote twenty-nine books, many of which were devoted to the study of the Shona or Mashona, the majority tribe of Zimbabwe, and their customs, religion, and culture. He was deeply impressed by the ethics of the Shona people, despite his admittedly racist views on African independence.

Eternally thinking, walking, doing, always on the verge of some limitless quest, Grandpa Mike could not tolerate a single unproductive moment and spent his time expounding on the topic of his work researching cures for subtropical African diseases. The previous year in America, he had set up a slide projector in the spare room to show my brother and me the stark images of those who suffered from the most dramatic of diseases native to subtropical Africa, the subjects of his research and care. Goiter. Elephantiasis.

Bilharzia.[4] Diseases that caused legs and necks to swell to disproportionately large sizes or blister painfully.

"Here is a man with goiter," my grandfather told us, clicking through slides. "And here is an image of elephantiasis," he remarked of another. Sheltered as I was then from disfiguring or chronic disease (or so I believed), these were distressing depictions. For my grandfather, however, these images were nothing short of revelatory. Colonial medicine practiced before 1950 in then-Rhodesia shunned the study of the effects of diseases on the African population, focusing instead on the prevention of diseases from which colonial whites suffered.

My grandfather, known for his research into bilharzia, a disease prevalent in tropical and sub-tropical areas in poor communities without potable water and adequate sanitation, was especially keen to recognize the symptoms in African children that the authorities had purposefully overlooked. Between giving important lectures that year in England, my grandfather grew exceedingly restless. One morning as he walked me to school, Grandpa Mike made a disturbing proposition. "Claire, why don't I give a lecture at your school on subtropical diseases?"

The student body of my school was comprised mainly of girls, three to twelve years old. I did not think the subject matter was appropriate. Worse than this, I faulted my grandfather for being in constant need of an audience. He would not take no for an answer and did his utmost to wear me down, beseeching me as we strolled past heaps of bright purple morning glories to let him speak to the headmistress. Despite his entreaties, somehow I managed to hold my ground.

---

4 Also known as schistosomiasis, this disease is spread by parasitic flatworms released by infected freshwater snails.

We didn't see much of my father over the next year and a half while my mother worked to establish herself as a barrister in criminal law. When he did manage to return home for the occasional week or two, he performed his domestic duties with ritualistic tenderness: making Saturday grocery trips to town by foot with the aid of the ubiquitous English wicker, handheld trolley; taking long strolls through the Epping Forest, where we climbed old pollard trees and meandered for hours along fecund streams; and playing board games with us children late into the night. I loved these games, particularly Monopoly, which I won handily almost every time. Our mother showed no interest whatsoever in our games, the shopping, or our long walks. She spent almost all of her time alone in her bedroom, studying or working, I presumed. It was really anyone's guess as to what she was doing up there.

Full Stop

One day during a class discussion of grammar and run-on sentences, our teacher, in a snarky mood, asked us to define what came at the end of a sentence. A regular "motor mouth," my hand shot immediately into the air.

"Period," I exclaimed loudly.

"Eww," the girls roared, turning in their seats to eye me with bemused horror, "that's disgusting."

"No, it's not," shouted our teacher over the classroom rumblings.

"What's wrong with the word *period*?" I asked, chafing at the divide between American and English culture. Our teacher was unable to tell me.

"Ask your mother," was the best she could offer. The term "full stop" was then discussed for a short moment before we returned to our lesson.

When she returned home from a long day at chambers, I asked my mother for the meaning of a "period."

"Once a month you have blue blood," Mom responded flippantly, chortling loudly for reasons I could not fully ascertain. Only after I asked my grandmother on one of her monthly visits, did I obtain a straight answer.

March 1975

It was in that detached townhouse on the edge of the Epping Forest that my mother entertained her boss, the head of a distinguished chambers and remote friend of her father's, who would eventually go on to become a Queen's Counsel, or judge. That early spring afternoon the house was filled with a bright winter light. I remember peeking in on my mother and her boss as they sat together in the living room: viewing his long thin legs crossed in the pinstriped pants of his profession, his pale complexion strikingly contrasted by the graying, immaculately coiffed hair. It wasn't common for my parents to invite people over, let alone colleagues. At the edge of a bright red and orange ombré shag rug, the stately looking employer sat in one of the chrome-framed white leather armchairs that my parents had had shipped with them from America. While my mother did very well hosting her superior for tea that afternoon, she would not succeed in maintaining her position at the chambers. After the initial trial period of six months was over, she was not rehired.

Very soon a dark pall fell over our home. My mother's class privilege would not be enough to protect her from certain injustices. She could not find a position at another chambers and grew more frantic with each passing month. One afternoon the phone rang in our downstairs hallway, and I made the unwitting mistake of answering. This was to be *that* fortune-changing call. The one final opportunity that was botched because of the rushed way I had answered the call. The rude inflection of my voice when I answered, "Hullo."

That afternoon on the carpeted floor of my bedroom, my mother unleashed her frustrations, sobbing, kicking and pummeling me for what felt like hours as the sun went down and the small room was engulfed in twilight. At ten years old, I had apparently lost my mother her final opportunity to flourish as a working professional. As the light of day churned into night, we would become inextricably bound by frustration, fear, and unparalleled rage.

"It is the strangest yellow, that wall-paper. It makes me think of all the yellow things I ever saw—not beautiful ones like buttercups, but old foul, bad yellow things. But there is something else about that paper—the smell! ... The only thing I can think of that it is like is the color of the paper! A yellow smell."

The Yellow Wallpaper
Charlotte Perkins Gilman

Like in Charlotte Perkins Gilman's feminist tale, our house on Hazelton Road soon took on the semblance of a tortured mind. As her prospects worsened and my mother teetered ever closer to the brink of psychosis, the walls of our northeastern London suburban home began to spring large, unforgiving cracks. We were soon to discover about our uniform subdivision of fifty or so houses that things were not as uniform as the developers had wanted us to believe. The result of an ill-conceived plan, our foursquare brick townhouse, set at the bottom of a sloping road, had been built over a small stream. During the winter rains, the stream became swollen, shifting the footings of our house's foundation that had been embedded in clay. By spring of the following year, the hairline cracks that had first appeared in the corners of each room began to swoop in horizontal branches across the walls.

The "optic horror" was all the proof my mother needed to sell the house back to the developer. Among our neighbors, my mother was the first to recognize the problem and the first to sell her home. With our full investment returned, my mother promptly set course back to America, where she would once again pursue a career in law inexplicably withheld from her in England.

3

a room with

a darker view

While her husband's career in astrophysics took him all around the globe, once again my mother hit the books. Returning to our tract home in Berkeley Heights that we rented out during our absence, in under a year she passed the New York bar, and then in another, the New Jersey bar. She would reinvent herself as an American criminal defense attorney, hoping to obtain the same elite standing in America as that of a criminal defense barrister in England. She simply ordered the right books, sequestered herself in a heavily draped bedroom and pored over the material day and night.

Again my mother struggled to find a permanent position. She was passed over for permanent hire at Legal Aid in Manhattan after a trial period of six months. Even when she offered her services for free, she was unable to maintain a position for long. Either she was not in possession of the right social skills or was considered too old, at thirty-seven, to be worthy of employment. I often wondered about my mother's struggle for social acceptance. Was it due to her age? Her immigrant background? Gender? An apparent lack of emotional affect?

Despite the demeaning lack of interest on the part of employers, she would continue to pursue a career in law. Shortly after being let go at Legal Aid, she opened an office in Brooklyn. It was in a building I would pass years later on the way from where I lived on Dean Street in Boerum Hill to the subway en route to New York University, where I was attending graduate school in creative writing. Glancing across the street from her former office, over my shoulder appeared the glinting gold statue of a blindfolded Lady Justice atop the Brooklyn Court Building, and I would consider my mother, wondering what justice there might be for her. Here in Brooklyn and from a second office in Jersey City, my mother worked as a court-appointed 18-B lawyer for adults facing criminal charges who could not afford a lawyer of their own, while helping undocumented immigrants apply for amnesty, a program implemented by President Carter in 1977.

Glass Ceiling Report

As it turned out, women's employment prospects in the U.S. legal field were not much more promising than in England. In the U.S., women have struggled historically to attain positions in large law firms. While today, according to a 2017 *Law360* Glass Ceiling report, women make up close to thirty-five percent of lawyers at firms and are still fighting for parity, the statistics were far worse for women looking for work in the same era as my mother was.[5] Cynthia Grant Bowman of Cornell Law School notes that it was only in the late-1970s when activist and feminist lawmaking demanded the enforcement of Title VII of the Civil Rights Act of 1964 that law firms began "to admit women into practice on allegedly equal terms with men... when (women) entered the profession in immense numbers, like a pent up stream."[6]

---

5 Bell, Jacqueline. "Women See Another Year Of Slow Gains At Law Firms – Law360." *Law360 – The Newswire for Business Lawyers*, Law360, July 2017. Web.

6 Bowman, Cynthia Grant. "Women in the Legal Profession from the 1920s to the 1970s: What Can We Learn from Their Experience About Law and Social Change." Cornell University Law School, Scholarship@Cornell Law: A Digital Repository, 2009. Web.

Bowman relates some astonishingly depressing statistics regarding the prospects of Jews, African-Americans, and women in law in the 1960s (my mother attended Oxford law school in the 1950s). Apparently, it was not uncommon for women to be ranked by recruiters to be the best candidates for entry-level positions only to be turned down by firms, who actively announced in interviews their preference for male candidates. Bowman relates, "What these women faced was encapsulated in a headline in the *Harvard Law Record* in December 1963, six months before their graduation: 'Women Unwanted.'" A survey of law firms reported in this article made it abundantly clear that women were rated the least desirable candidates, beneath the lower half of the graduating class in men, and lower than that of African-Americans. "The reasons firms supplied for their negative rating of women candidates included: 'Women can't keep the pace'; 'bad relationships with the courts'; 'responsibility is in the home'; and 'afraid of emotional outbursts'," Bowman cites.[7]

To bump headlong into statistics that point to the routine denial of the employment of African-Americans as a means for explicating the difficulties white women faced attaining work is bracing at best, and at worst indicative of rampant societal bias. Apparently being Jewish in the 1960s was also a liability. Bowman relays, quoting sociologist Erwin Smigel, "'Women are discriminated against to a greater degree than are Jews.' NYU reported that 90 percent of the law firms contacting its placement office refused even to interview women."[8]

---

7 Ibid.

8 Ibid.

Late 1970s

My mother's attempt to find employment during the giddy years of the late 1970s had unsurprisingly failed. She was never going to be "one of the guys" and probably had little access to a female mentor. Despite her slim prospects, she published her appeals in the New Jersey and New York *Law Journal*, the thick paperbound books that piled up in dizzying stacks about the study, her bedroom, the dining room, everywhere around the house much like the thick white astrophysics journals that would arrive for my father each month. These appeals were written on behalf of indigent clients who were accused of burglary, rape, and a variety of other crimes, whose civil rights may have been violated in one way or another. Publication did not result in convictions being overturned necessarily. Toward the end of her career, my brother relayed the dismaying story of a final offer of employment. A top divorce lawyer, Raoul Felder, had hired my mother for very low wages to run errands and run the Xerox machine. Rather than perform these less than desirable duties, and under the influence of a persistent psychosis, she spent her afternoons at the bank checking on her accounts, convinced she was being robbed.

Despite a career being of great importance to my mother, on the subject of relationships between the sexes, she often made baffling, contradictory statements. She would say, *I should have married a rich man when I had the chance.* Or, *I can't be bothered with housewives. They are far too boring.* When she went back to work, the neighborhood women were designated the enemy. They were all suspect, too trite to engage with.

The remedy would have been to establish ties with working women. This, however, seemed far from her mind. Beyond the one woman with whom she shared an office briefly, there was no mention of working with women, of a fruitful solidarity with a displaced and dismissed gender, as far as I recall. As many of my college-aged students today report of their own homes, feminism was not a term used in our household.

Latchkey kids

Shortly after our return from England in 1976, my brother John and I had become quintessential latchkey kids. After my mother's disappointment with nannies and sitting services, we were left to our own devices. When we were not in school, we were restricted to playing by ourselves at home. Friends were not allowed in our yard. Overly conscious of a litigious society, our mother was convinced we would be sued if anyone were hurt. Impossible strictures, we rebelled with the anticipated negative consequences.

Over time my mother's rules became more and more stringent. I was rarely allowed to socialize, and my overt rebellion was of great concern. It didn't help that in junior high I was somehow accidentally tracked with a group of students who had no intention of graduating from high school. Hanging around after school with my classmates, whose academic failure carried no repercussions at home, I began acting accordingly. Cutting classes. Drinking in the woods. Shoplifting. At the end of eighth grade, my mother's recourse was to have me enrolled in a private all-girls school. It was clear from my extracurricular activities that I had lost my way.

My new school came as a welcome relief from the overwhelming confusion of a large public school where differences were openly derided and bullying was acceptable practice. At Kent Place, academic expectations were much higher, camaraderie more easily attained, and socializing less fraught with peril. The one peculiarity of this institution was the vocal and persistent sense of superiority on the part of the student body. While commuting between our small suburban homes on the trains and in the train station, it was not uncommon for private school students to comment on the attire and diction of the public school students as inherently inferior. By virtue of our entrance into a private school, which was based more on financial capabilities than other criteria, we were of an elevated stock. A gross sense of entitlement permeated the place.

"Senseless laughter"

As I commuted back and forth by train the short distance between Berkeley Heights and Summit, to the only all-girls non-parochial day school in the state, proudly underperforming during the day (ecstatically listening to the early rap music of The Sugar Hill Gang on my small Panasonic radio late into the night), my mother knocked herself out working long days, leaving the house before seven not to return until seven or eight at night. The difficult commute back and forth between Manhattan, Brooklyn, and Jersey City began to take its toll. My mother's sleep patterns became more and more erratic. Sleeping less and less, often turning in to bed at midnight with a cup of hot instant coffee in her hand to rise as early as 3 a.m., before, finally, she stopped sleeping altogether.

Alone and unprovoked, my mother would laugh uninter-rupted for hours at a time. In the evening after work, she would stand in the small downstairs bathroom adjacent to the rec room, where my brother and I languished mawkishly before the television set, and stare in the mirror, gazing and laughing as if responding to the most hilarious joke. I always imagined that these marathon sessions were when she played out rich revenge scenarios, in which she was Manhattan's reigning legal mind. The "senseless laughter" became a regular feature of our home life. In the midst of great bouts of laughter, my mother would lie in bed for hours at a time among a sea of legal briefs and books. The unceasing hilarity would reverberate throughout the chaotically furnished, two-story tract home.

Whenever I was on the telephone (another forbidden act), if my mother was in the midst of one of these inexplicable bouts, the door to her bedroom shut, I would stretch the long cord of the kitchen phone into the hallway to catch the sound of her laughter over the receiver. This was as far as the long coiled yellow cord would reach. From here, whoever was on the other end of the line would assent: *Yes, I hear her.* I would then try to find words for what I could not explain and had yet to understand. *She's really neurotic,* I would say, committing an act of extreme disloyalty. *No you don't understand. She's really, really neurotic.*

.

Generational divide

My mother took her profession seriously, buying the latest suits each Fall at Saks Fifth Avenue in Millburn or Lord & Taylor in Short Hills and favoring blue tweed and tan corduroy. She seemed to have multiples of each in her large walk-in closet. These suits varied in the length or flare of the skirt or the width of the corduroy band. I evaluated these clothes on a regular basis, somewhat envious.

My wardrobe paled by comparison if not for the simple reason that, at thirteen, my mother deemed me too fat to warrant the purchase of new clothes. Perhaps this would have been impetus for me to lose weight if I suffered from a weight problem. But this was hardly the case. I was five-foot six and weighed 132 pounds. In light of my mother's pronouncement, my father took up the task of clothing his children. Unmoved by fashion or material acquisition in general, my father took my brother and me to Korvette's, a forerunner of the big box store, to purchase our clothes. The shopping trips felt sour to me, as I had always equated Korvette's and Route 22, its location, with the purchase of tires and other such unglamorous goods. At some point we graduated to the Livingston Mall, where we purchased lava lamps and hypnotic black velvet posters. Here Dad would grow annoyed if I didn't shop the discounted rack. "Why can't you buy something on sale?" he would say. Further proof of his lukewarm feelings for us, I determined, tainted by 1970s run-amok capitalism.

A strong generational divide existed between us. Unfamiliar with scarcity, we found our parent's disinterest in material goods confounding. Having grown up during the blitzkrieg, my father was unaccustomed to the demands of a throwaway society. Whenever my brother and I insisted on the purchase of new clothes, from where he sat, my father would lift a shoe for us to get a close view of its bottom, repeating the same discouraging mantra: *I've worn these shoes for fifteen years. Fifteen years. Why do you need new shoes?* And yes, it was true. Under the thinning leather sole of his right shoe appeared the slow beginnings of a hole. My father was that classic clichéd scientist type. He uncomplainingly wore whatever his mother sent to him from England—the wide-legged polyester pants, stiff button-down shirts with the useful front pocket, year after year. Later when he began research on a telescope of his design atop Mauna Kea, much to the chagrin of the native Hawaiian population who did not condone building on their sacred summit, but who would eventually be coaxed into relinquishing their land rights for jobs promised in numbers that never materialized, he began purchasing Hawaiian shirts like other CalTech scientists. He tended to favor a bright orange one, which I found puzzling. With dazzling sapphire eyes, a crop of wavy dark hair, my father looked most dashing in any shade of blue.

My father's unfettered climb in his field, in an era when scientific research was highly regarded and well funded, meant there was never a fear of impending financial shortages. It was this security that afforded my mother her foray into a less than remunerative self-employment. As her illness escalated, my father would often return from California, or wherever else it was he had been, to find a staggering heap of unopened mail on the black tile of the foyer floor. My father would go ballistic once he opened the mail. The bank statements were a special sticking point.

"I can't believe it, Joy," he would shout. "You are $7,000 into PACE again."

PACE, I came to learn, was the acronym for an account that extended my parents an automatic credit line once their checking account had a negative balance. My father was hopping mad, and my mother had no trouble laughing this off. She almost seemed to relish these moments.

1970–1981

As time passed, my mother grew more frantic. Her driving was terrible. Not that it had ever been passable. Earlier, when we lived in England, my father had tried teaching her to drive a stick shift to no avail. Those Saturday afternoons were spent in the back seat, with the car lurching suddenly, as my mother struggled to put the unspectacular green

English sedan into gear. No matter the number of lessons, she never improved, until finally, they gave up on the whole enterprise. Her movements were then limited to, fortunate for her, the excellent British mass transit system.

In America, when we were in grade school, she drove in a state of tense panic, slowly drifting to straddle the center lines of our hilly town's small roads. Fearful of crashing her car, she maintained a speed well under the twenty-five-miles-per-hour limit, causing visible consternation on the part of the other drivers, our neighbors. Angry beeping was not out of the ordinary. My brother and I would duck down in the back seat, mortified, hoping to go unrecognized, while my mother steadily navigated her young wards in the direction of home. A town of under ten thousand inhabitants, nestled in the Watchung Mountains and just six or so square miles in area, there were thankfully few cars on the road.

My mother's morning commute began with the short two-mile drive to the downtown train station. She had to leave earlier than she would have wanted; the commute on the various train lines—the Morris-Essex train lines to Newark and PATH to New York City, the Erie L. from B.H. to Hoboken, trains to Brooklyn, back to Manhattan or to Jersey City, depending upon her schedule—had to be timed precisely. In the winter months, her commute was made even more grueling by the inclement weather and the many blizzards. My mother would often leave us behind on snow days, when she ruled it too dangerous for us to attend schools even as she hazarded the icy roads for the courtrooms of the city. Mornings were always difficult. Inevitably she would shout out in desperation, *Where are my keys?* or, *I can't find my comb!* My brother would dutifully find them for her, always to my chagrin.

"Why do you help her?" I would deride him for aiding and abetting "the enemy." I had long since bowed out from participating in her wellbeing.

"It's easier to help than not," my brother explained, expounding a brand of pragmatism I would not come to understand until much later. More than this, my mother treated her second-born with a little more gentle reserve. This would be to her great benefit as it was my brother who would, at the prompting of my mother's father, take on the role of dutiful caregiver that her illness required.

Singular solution

One winter morning I recall my mother struggling with a typical adversity. The garage door, as a consequence of the fluctuating temperatures of the previous day, was frozen shut. The snow that melted had formed a powerful seal of ice between the mechanical garage door and the cement floor. My mother's usual remedy was to heat water in a small pot on the stove and then pour it over the seal to help melt the ice. On this particular occasion she did not have time to heat a pot of water. She may not have expected the appearance of the ice. Or she may have been busy ironing creases out of her suit jacket or skirt that morning, leaving her less time to address the hindrance.

For whatever reason, that day my mother determined a singular solution to her winter troubles. She got into the front seat of her subcompact car, running the engine before putting it into reverse, successfully barreling through the heavy wood garage door, splintering it into many pieces, all in an effort to get to the train station on time. Her determination to show up in court, to come through on behalf of her clients, clearly knew no bounds.

Like my mother, I had trouble maintaining my morning schedule of travel on the N.J. transit Morris-Essex train line. Never leaving the house in time to walk the mile-and-a-half through the woods behind our house and down Plainfield Avenue to the train station, I was habitually late and found myself sprinting the final three blocks whenever I heard the whistle of an approaching train.

Once, I inadvertently boarded the same train car as my mother. I had left the house a daring time-shaving two or three minutes later than usual and missed my regular train. I had looked forward to bantering and smoking with school friends during the short fifteen minutes between train stops. Worse than missing my train, however, I made the error of boarding an express train that did not stop in Summit. My mother must have been late to work that morning too, and for some reason, I had failed to see her on the platform. Perhaps she had been waiting in her car for the train, steeling herself from the freezing cold outside.

Adding to my predicament, I had absconded with a blouse of my mother's that I was expressly forbidden from wearing. Terrified of being caught, I fastened my coat tightly, and took the empty seat next to hers. My mother glanced in my direction momentarily, and then turned away as if I were a complete stranger, apparently more disturbed by my presence than I hers. This came as a small relief. However, after the train failed to stop in Summit and I discovered that I had boarded the express train for Newark, I found myself in need of my mother's expertise. A privileged girl of the suburbs, I felt a certain trepidation approaching a city stereotyped for little more than a high crime rate. Except on school field trips to the Empire State Building or World

Trade Center, at fifteen years old I had never ventured farther outside of my alarmingly white enclave other than to the moneyed suburbs of Bernardsville or Millburn. While I was of a less elite background than the wealthier set of girls who went on annual ski trips to Switzerland and Vail, and who summered in Martha's Vineyard or belonged to The Lake Club, owned condos in Florida, or "showed" on $50,000 horses on weekends, I was still fairly insulated from life outside of anything other than middle class 1970s suburbia.

This loud train ride along thumping rails was to be the furthest I had ventured outside the rosy ring of leafy suburban privilege. My mother, however, declined to help me navigate the large and unfamiliar terrain of the Newark train station with its hefty number of tracks into which we pulled shortly after passing a long tract of foreboding tall brick tenements. Deboarding in Newark, awed by the array of train lines, I eventually managed to board the correct train for Summit, arriving at school over two hours late. Later that night I discovered the reason that my mother had ignored my presence on the train—I had made her appear "old."

My mother's struggles at work weren't limited to shallow first impressions. She also suffered enormously over inter-personal communication. Whenever my professionally smooth-sailing father was home, my mother would take full advantage of his expertise and acumen. Bombarding my father nightly at the dinner table with her troubles, it became clear that something was wrong. She would often retell the same story in precise detail, asking him to divine for her the meaning of a reaction or response of a colleague or judge, for hours. *What do you think he meant?* she would repeatedly ask, never content with the response. Eventually my father would forgo reason or conjecture for a simple answer—*I don't know, Joy. I don't know.*

In fact, she rarely sat down at the table with us unless it was to work him over on the subject of her professional angst. She didn't partake in meals. She was on a perpetual diet, subsisting almost exclusively on snack-size Slim Jims, frozen meat patties, cottage cheese, and Tab. Low-calorie Kavli crackers with margarine were another source of sustenance. These fraught mealtime conversations would eventually end in loud shouting matches. On one occasion in a fit of rage, after he overturned the kitchen table, sending the dishes flying, my father stomped off into the garage to return to work. An hour later I found my father still in the garage, seated behind the steering wheel of his car, gazing absently into the gloom.

Illness and its demands

An intense secrecy was integral to my mother's survival. She knew better than to communicate her anxieties and fears to anyone outside the home. It had been years since she had eliminated frank conversation with neighbors or anyone else. Her immediate family was a safe place to unload her doubts, along with her fantastic renderings of the world-at-large. As the demands for secrecy grew more severe entering the spring trimester of my tenth grade, I started to suffer from overpowering feelings of hopelessness and despair. I was a disappointment to my parents and highly cynical about academic achievement.

My father had done his best to cultivate a sense of family on the weekends when we were younger, but this became less tenable as the demands of his work intensified: the telescope being built in Hawaii, one of the very few in the world of its kind; the flying in NASA airplanes at Moffett Field in Northern California with delicate submillimeter radio instruments; and a new professorship at CalTech. We became less and less a family. And, as my mother's chaos grew to consume our home—with law briefs stacked all about, expensive clothes strewn everywhere, hair dye splattered over the bathroom walls, and dirty dishes and mail left to mount—cleaning up after her began to feel like an all-consuming job.

It also never ceased to amaze me how little sustenance she would provide my brother and me. Her shopping was geared almost entirely toward her needs. For us, there might be some frozen FoodTown pizzas, a bag of Mars chocolate bars, and maybe a few cans of Dinty More stew, Chef Boyardee ravioli, or Spaghetti-os. After cleaning all morning one Saturday, I took it upon myself to rail at her—

a predictable tirade that did precious little to change our situation.

In the 1970s, mental illness was rarely openly discussed. At a time when anorexia was euphemistically referred to as a "worm," I had little in the way of cultural markers to define the trouble brewing in our home. Had there been complex representations of these illnesses on television as on those popular shows today—for example, *Homeland*'s Carrie, who has a bipolar condition, or Dr. Walter Bishop's self-induced schizophrenia on *Fringe*—I might have been able to advocate for my mother and help her to obtain treatment. Instead, my family and I missed the very common hallmark signs of the disease. As it stealthily progressed, we grew used to its strange permutations, making odd justifications for its intensifying demands.

Mrs. Harvilchuck

At some point during my sophomore year, I started experimenting with pills, taking some variation on the fabled "black beauties" of a bygone era. Touted as a powerful amphetamine, in actuality these weak pills sold to privileged naïve teenagers were probably just ground caffeine pressed into small black gelatin capsules. I don't recall where I got them, only that after taking them they offered a mild kick at best.

That year in English class we were given a short creative assignment, and I decided to try my hand at confessional writing. I knew what I was doing, perhaps better than I do now with all of my adult commitments and material entrapments. I downed some pills, called a friend on the forbidden telephone, locked myself in the basement away from my mother's paranoid surveillance, and became overwrought. I then scrawled onto lined paper my feelings of self-loathing and disadvantage, reflecting on the perks and privileges of the girls who appeared happier and more stable, whose family miseries were not yet on full display, and handed it in to our teacher, Mrs. Harvilchuck, who, with her impossibly high standards, routinely caused the less analytical among us to melt down.

This same teacher who once humiliated me during class by demanding that I stop pretending to be stupid when I admitted feeling confounded in the face of eighteenth-century poetry, came to find me one afternoon in our student lounge, with the paper I had submitted folded vertically in half, like all of our graded papers. Passing it back to me, she said she wanted to publish it in the school paper.

"You must come for a conference. We should discuss this."

I never did seek out that meeting, nor did I vie for that publication.

Bernardsville

Visits to a friend's nineteenth-century English rural stone house in Bernardsville, a former summer colony for Gilded Age industrialists and financiers, were the highlight of my high school years. Here, my friend and I rode horses, swam in the neighbor's pool, and on occasion visited other school friends at the nearby "Lake Club." We would drink apple-flavored whiskey and swim in the cool lake, then climb back into the light blue Volkswagen Rabbit to return to the house, where my friend's mother would have spent the day gardening before preparing a delicious Waldorf salad for us.

The tenor of life in this home could not have been more opposite to mine. The overstuffed furniture, decorated in bright yellow and green floral patterns, reeked of old money. The floors were a rich oak, the cold stone of the walls so different from the hollow drywall of my home. From iron casement windows throughout the long narrow home, the views were of rolling fields and elegant mature oaks. Antique wood vanities and dressers graced the corners of each of the small bedrooms. When my teenage companion was in trouble, it was for something inarguable and concrete. *You used my sewing scissors to cut flowers. How could you?* my friend's mom might charge. An infraction so light and frivolous it seemed almost a compliment.

Even more exciting were the times when the Kirklands went away for the weekend and we would invite teenage boys over and drink. These occasional forays edging into sexual intimacy were fraught with peril. No one asked to visit me at home, but what would happen if I established stronger ties with a boy from another school? How would I explain my chaotic home life to someone who grew up in an eighteenth-century stone mansion? I knew better than to entertain rescue fantasies. After dabbling some, I drew strong boundaries. Inevitably, flirtations remained in the nascent stages of desire.

Southern California, 1978

The summer before tenth grade, my brother and I spent a couple of weeks with our father in California, where he had rented a two-bedroom in a featureless stucco apartment building on South Wilson Avenue in Pasadena, which was walking distance from his job. While Dad worked in a nondescript building on California Boulevard, we could be found across the street at the palm lined CalTech pool, basking in an unfamiliar calm.

California was as sunny as it was purported to be. Each morning I woke up to a relentlessly blue sky. I was as shocked by the climate as I was stunned by the abundance of luxury vehicles darting between freeway lanes. Apparently, everyone here was rich or at least eager to appear that way. Pasadena was nothing like the East Coast. Large Mission-style and Greene & Greene houses were set unimaginably close to the sidewalk and hardly a distance apart in Pasadena. No one owned a mansion or even a large house in northern New Jersey unless it was set on six acres or more of property. And in New Jersey, before the explosion of Wall Street in the 1990s, the wealthy typically cloaked their money driving modest cars like Volkswagen Rabbits or mid-sized Volvos. Here in Los Angeles people zipped about in the latest top of the line Mercedes or BMW.

I wasn't convinced at first that I liked California more than the East, but I certainly welcomed the change.

As summer dragged on, my mother persevered in publishing and winning multiple appeals. She would often have me read them out loud to her so she could contemplate her outpourings. These appeals were written by hand on long sheets of yellow legal paper. As I recall, the writing was severely repetitious, as if the copy and paste of the personal computer age had already been invented. This early exposure to the writing of appeals cured me of any interest in pursuing a career in law. This and the hardships my mother endured.

Of these repetitious tomes, two of her appeals made a lasting impression. One was the rape appeal that I was expressly forbidden to read. Naturally I availed myself of this murky, disturbing read right away. It was hardly the best introduction to sex. But I can't say it was in any way worse an introduction than the reading of *The Fan Club*, a pulp novel by Irvine Wallace, that I found among my father's books in the spare room, detailing the kidnapping and somewhat sickening gang rape of a "famous actress," who eventually secures her own release through the preposterous telegraphing of her signature body measurements: 36-24-34. The other appeal gave me insight into social inequalities hinged upon racial profiling. The defendant was of Arab descent, and the incriminating evidence of this liquor store robbery included a brown paper bag and a screwdriver. The main argument of the appeal rested on an unwarranted search. Despite the fact that my mother had stopped sleeping almost entirely, she was completely capable of performing on behalf of her clients.

While my mother continued to strive, my own ambition for success was nothing short of anemic. I wanted nothing more than the swift passage of time so that I might leave my family for college, any college. Course work didn't interest me. All that mattered was that I could get away.

Guidance counselor

The rift between my mother and I intensified as the accusations escalated. On an almost weekly basis, I was accused of being a tart, of being on an official police list of prostitutes, of desiring my father sexually. This wasn't entirely new. From the time I was eight or nine, my mother would often say alarming things to me apropos of nothing. *Without your eyes or hair, you have nothing,* she would exhort. Years after this, her mantra changed: *Never let a boy stick himself inside of you.* She had no filter. The dark, painful thoughts that plagued her were ascribed to anyone and everyone without mediation. She demanded that my father and I not sit so closely together on the couch. Any contact I had with him was suspect, and I was routinely humiliated by her accusations when he would return home for markedly briefer and briefer periods.

In a feeble attempt to find some relief, I began regularly seeing the guidance counselor at school. I found it difficult to describe my troubled home to this proper-looking woman in the preppy garb of a pale-yellow Fair-Isle sweater and kelly-green headband. Even more off-putting was the family photograph displayed prominently on her desk, reflecting back to me my outsider status. In this photo, our guidance counselor appeared with the math teacher, a notoriously recalcitrant man, with their eight neatly groomed children, conjoined Brady Bunch-style into one household from previous marriages. How would I explain to this raging success of family life the torments that afflicted my own blood ties? How would she react to stories of my mother's incandescent rage? The unrelenting accusations? Bouts of manic laughter? The sloth? Anti-social behavior? To my defensive maneuvers? What if she knew the truth of my family's near disdain for material acquisition? At that tender age, I wanted the trappings of the happy suburban life. I knew better than to reveal our flaws to this stranger. Even so, I knew the overpowering feelings of hopelessness and despair that plagued me were not reasonable. They threatened to take me under. This counselor, however conservative, was the best hope I had for staying afloat.

Winter & Spring trimesters, 1980

A month or so after a number of meetings with my counselor, my father was called to come speak to her. My parents's response to the school counselor's request was both aggressive and unhappy. Living primarily in California, my father had either returned specifically to handle this mess, or had been ambushed by the call while on one of his monthly visits. He was not pleased, and this displeasure emanated from his tense grip on the steering wheel as he drove me to school that morning in his green Cutlass Supreme. Descending Morris Avenue for Summit, the trees almost in bloom, I was overcome with such anxiety that I experienced a gut-wrenching knot in my stomach so intense I had to slip out from the bucket seat down to the floor of the car, unable to maintain a seated position. I had never experienced pain like this before. What did I fear? A negative report on my academic performance? I was a difficult student in need of attention. I wasn't sure what my counselor might say about me.

My time with her had included a certain amount of test taking. At first she gave me a straightforward IQ test. Maybe she needed to eliminate the possibility that I was either a misunderstood genius or severely limited in my intellectual capacities. I received a score of 135, a number that I determined to be low, particularly when considering my family's high expectations. During these hours together, she soon tried passing off the Rorschach inkblot test as another IQ test; the Rorschach, ironically enough, had originally been designed to help diagnose schizophrenia. I had no fear of the results, for I had made up my mind at a very young age, perhaps as early as five, that my mind would never become derailed in the same fashion as my mother's. I believed I had a choice. I believed I could establish boundaries between mental realms that I planned never to cross. For this reason, I did not balk at the intrusive testing. Instead I welcomed the attention, the calm hours seated on the comfortable couch in her office.

That dreaded day

Dumb luck would place me in the downstairs hallway of the main building when my father left the counselor's office. I was probably returning from the cafeteria when I caught sight of him on his way out. With his brown leather briefcase in hand, he looked angry, tense. This intervention, arranged on the part of my counselor, had clearly not gone well.

When I returned home that evening, my father disclosed the conversation. My less-than-stellar academic performance was probably up for discussion, but I have no memory of this. What followed was a shared joke between my parents. Apparently, as my father relayed to my mother, the counselor's main concern was that I didn't think my mother loved me. My parents shared a hardy laugh over this. I had never considered my counselor to be particularly bright, and this remark was all the proof I needed.

My mother had never expressed a pronounced ability to love. It made no sense to look to her for a show of emotional support or warmth. She was never demonstrative, effusive, beguiled by any one of us; therefore, I did not expect this kind of exchange from her. I simply sought relief from an ongoing hazard that I could not easily articulate.

My father tried to cajole me into feeling better about my home life. He told me the problems I had at fifteen, that seemed so big and insurmountable, would later seem very insignificant indeed. I had an exaggerated view of my unhappiness, he explained to me. He was seated on the long brown plaid couch I had on more than one occasion lit a match to in order to witness the distressing sight of globby, melting manmade fibers.

That night my mother and father were united in their good humor, a rarity. From that day forward, my mother added another caveat to her morning ritual. *You mustn't say any-thing to your teachers about us,* she would shout through my closed bedroom door, before clacking down the polished wood stairs in low black heels for her white Chevy Vega, the train station, and whichever court she was due in that day.

I began to threaten my mother with anything I could get my hands on: long carving knives, a small plastic bottle of liquid plant fertilizer. I threatened to slit her throat, to lace her coffee with poison when her back was turned. *I am going to kill you if you keep this up,* I would threaten cruelly, knowing I could never exact such revenge against my mother.

My mother kept up the melodrama, hiding the carving knives in plain sight in a cabinet high above the oven in an open bid to maintain her safety. She must have known I would not carry out my threats. My father would come home intermittently from his world travels and demand to know what happened to the carving knives whenever he was preparing a meal for the family, a duty my mother had long since given up. *Joy,* he would shout from downstairs, *where are the knives?*

We would then hear our mother's bedroom door open as she proceeded for the kitchen in a see-through nylon nightgown or something equally discomfiting, laughing mildly over the strained drama.

"I hid them from Claire," she would say rising up on her tippy-toes, to retrieve the long, sharp utensils from the cabinet. Rooted to the dingy, flecked white linoleum floor, my father would watch wordlessly.

What was he to make of this barbarous family of his?

With Ronald Reagan's ascent to the presidency, I felt myself even more at odds with those in charge of my private school education. Having just finished reading in our junior year Richard Hofstadter's *The United States: The History of a Republic*, with its clear delineation of the failure of Herbert Hoover's "trickle-down" economic policy and the resulting 1929 Depression, it seemed more than obvious that Reagan's widely lauded supply-side economic policy was a recipe for disaster. Weren't we studying history to learn from our mistakes?

Our teacher, Ms. J., was married to a Wall Street stockbroker and failed to draw any connection between the Depression, "the trickle-down theory," and Reagan's campaign platform. My questions along these lines were blankly dismissed.

Expulsion

When she wasn't insisting the district attorney was hiding behind our house in the bushes spying on her, my mother was accusing me of taking the train into Manhattan on weekends to sell him her secrets. It was a powerful delusion over which I had no control. Inevitably, these flights of mania were followed by ceaseless bouts of laughter. My reckless behavior intensified in concert with her psychosis. We were always at odds, fighting over small things, like whether I could visit friends on the weekends, what have you. Meanwhile, I was breaking many rules at school, smoking, and engaging in other teenage nonsense.

By the end of my junior year, I finally succeeded in loosening myself from my mother's care. This came as a relief; I could not see a future for myself on the East Coast. Whenever I tried imagining myself living in a New Jersey suburb, the other half of a happy procreating couple, I would see myself falling from a map of the Eastern Seaboard into the Atlantic Ocean. After engineering an ignoble departure, I went to live with my father in Pasadena. This much-needed outcome was precipitated by an exuberant amount of drinking during the Christmas Pageant, which resulted in my puking out one of the windows of our second-story Junior class lounge, streaking the white exterior of the faux Tudor building with chunks of partially digested pizza and debauching my hapless counselor's air conditioner.

4

and it was running thin

In Southern California, I was finally able to get some breathing room. I was no longer tethered to the 1970s and endless tributes to The Doors and Led Zeppelin. In Pasadena, home to surfer-friendly New Wave radio station KROQ, I not only stepped into the light, so to speak, but also into the present day. The techno '80s.

I imagine that the person who suffered most at this juncture was my brother. Alone in New Jersey, John had no choice but to keep my mother going, despite the worsening of her condition and her increasing symptoms. Less capable of doing things for herself, she knew my departure was a condemnation of some sort, an indication that something was indisputably wrong. She took my defection badly, and as punishment, tossed my small library of paperback books—literary classics, agit-prop, and supermarket pulps: Saul Bellow, Graham Greene, Philip Roth, Kurt Vonnegut, V.C. Andrews, Stephen King, Asimov, Leon Uris, Ayn Rand, Herman Wouk—from my bedroom bookcase into the trash.

While my father spent his time at CalTech completing the designs for the Mauna Kea submillimeter radio telescope, I attended Blair High School, one of California's fabled, troubled institutions. Its open-air-plan, abutting the Arroyo Seco Parkway—considered the country's first freeway, and a close neighbor of a hulking power plant—suffered from the lack of oversight and rampant neglect associated with white flight from the public school system that came along with mandatory busing and desegregation in the 1970s.

Little was being taught in these classrooms. Whites were in the minority. Racial tensions ran high, but were especially pronounced between Latino and African-American students. The after-school "race wars" were legendary. On one side of

Marengo Avenue, the young male Latino students would gather in the customary garb of chinos and white undershirts; the black students, similarly shirted but in jeans, lined up on the other side of the street with chains and fiberglass nunchucks, while the white kids—heirs to Spanish-style and Greene & Greene homes, with their San Marino girlfriends and other elite privileges—slipped safely out of the parking lot in Volkswagen Rabbits, Jeeps, vintage collectibles, sensible Toyotas, averting their eyes from the daily tensions that erupted between the gangs. Education being entirely stratified, AP classes were almost exclusively white but for one or two African-American or Asian students.

Pasadena was, in short, a powerful microcosm of racial inequality in America. By the end of my senior year, reading Engels along with a like-minded friend, I had become a budding Marxist.

1981–1982

School seemed less and less important. I ditched class with friends whenever I could, cruising in my best friend's 1970s red Mustang along the Linda Vista neighborhood's wide avenues lined with orange trees, lounging about in houses that were mid-century modern, or Spanish-style adobe, bingeing on fast food or beer. When it rained, we would drive into the foothills of Altadena for the snow-topped San Gabriel Mountains on a seventy-five-degree day in January to haul back the frozen rewards of nature, in order to peg the hot waspy guys with snowballs. I always marveled at these entitled, polo shirt-wearing surfers. What had they done to deprive themselves of the elite private school education almost all middle-class aspirants opted for? What infractions might they have committed? Perhaps their parents had simply chosen expensive cars over children's educations, as one friend would report.

Meanwhile, my mother's condition continued to deteriorate, to the point that she could no longer determine her child's identity. Suffering from Capgras syndrome, a delusionary psychological state, she would call to tell me she thought my brother was an imposter: *I don't think John is John anymore,* she would confide in a worn, tired voice. *He has hair on his legs.* Or she would surprise me by announcing how she saw me on television that day. *Was that you on Channel Seven?* she would ask.

It soon became apparent to my father that he needed to help my brother move out to California. No sooner did he begin to help my brother, then my mother decided that she was ready to move to California, too. This came as a surprise. No one expected her to give up her law practice, ever. But she might have sensed that without my brother's close presence, she would not be able to cope. The work had clearly become too much for her, the untreated illness an insurmountable burden. She might have also sensed that she was on the brink of an annihilating abandonment. Without her family to confide in about her delusions and hallucinations, how would she survive? Her family was her anchor, if nothing else. It was not clear to me why no one tried to get her help.

Years later, my father would confide in me that it was too difficult to have anyone committed then against his or her will, particularly a capable lawyer. Without her consent, treatment would have been impossible .

What mattered to me then was protecting my father and myself from further misery. He had a girlfriend he was serious about, and I was convinced that I would not survive another moment of this misshapen parental union. When the news hit of my mother's impending move to California, I demanded that my father consider his options seriously.

"You cannot live with her again. You will be miserable," I argued, adding the following caveat: "You won't be able to continue on with your life as it is now."

It was clear to me that my father had moved on, in all senses of the word. Like me, my father had been the target of my mother's harangues, particularly as she suffered greater and crueler frustrations at work. I didn't see why my mother, whom I deemed to be neurotic and spiteful, should heap more misery upon us. Tragically, I had yet to understand that she suffered from a condition that required treatment. All I knew was that I needed at least one fairly happy, functioning parent to ensure my own survival. My father was an excellent provider in the sense that he was on a firm, assured path. While I fought bitterly with my father—disappointed in not having won his easy approval— the worsening of my mother's condition, the gendered competition, and her angry bouts of paranoia rendered her unredeemable in my eyes.

At seventeen years old, I wanted a life of my own. I wanted a home to return to from college where the battle lines drawn between the sexes were not paramount. My mother's presence would make that impossible. Like many adolescent girls, I saw my father in more glowing light than I did my mother, who, unlike my father, did not jet to foreign lands on special assignment, bestowing upon me, his besotted little girl, glittering objects from airport terminal stores. My father, I believed, lacked backbone when it came to his strident and unpredictable wife. He needed to stand up for himself and his right to a loving home. He needed to assert himself not just for his own sake, but for my brother's and mine too.

Summer 1982

When it was decided that I would be going to San Francisco State University, my father deemed my ruin complete.

"My poor Claire," he said, as he embraced me.

This response amounted to self-fulfilling prophecy. I had the proof I had been looking for all along. Academic success would be the one and only measure of my worth. Early on, I had determined my parents's workaholic habits and my mother's strange strictures as inhumane. I could not comprehend her lack of social contact and disinterest in even the most minimal aspects of homemaking. But I was too young to appreciate the complexities facing the many women who had the dual hopes of caring for a family while meaningfully taking part in the outside world. My mother's mother had spent her every moment tending to the needs of a husband whose ceaseless work as a doctor, teacher, writer, and editor in his field of subtropical medicine kept them both exceedingly busy and for the most part, in an academic limelight. What did her mother have to teach her about a professional life? Or balancing that professional life with parental duties?

Even though my mother's undiagnosed behavior stirred

in me feelings of rebelliousness, she was not the sole cause of my disaffection; she worked hard on my behalf when she believed I had taken my rebellion too far. In middle school, when my truant behavior became excessive, she demanded that my father send me to private school. Later when my PSAT scores turned out to be less than impressive, my mother signed me up for a weekend SAT study course, extraordinary then, common now among competitive elites. My ultimately reasonable scores, coupled with my disastrously low grade-point average, made it possible for me to attend what was declared by the Yale Book of Colleges to be the best state school in California.

At $333 a semester, my undergraduate education at San Francisco State University was an incredible bargain. My father knew I might not have the same opportunities as he did with an Oxford education, but he also knew better than to slag on the fabled city. When my father took me to San Francisco to find housing that August, I insisted he pay for my best friend, Gari, to come with me, as support. I could count on Gari, the oldest of three and another transplant from Berkeley Heights, New Jersey to So Cal, to manage the details, even if she was only eighteen years old.

As we drove through Daly City for the fogbound Outer Sunset, Dad suddenly remarked, "If you don't like San Francisco, you have no soul."

My ears pricked up. Never before had my materialist father remarked on the numinous.

My father finalized his divorce from my mother the year that I left for college. I rented a room in a third floor Victorian flat on Pine Street, two blocks from Divisidero Street in the Western Addition, a primarily African-American neighborhood then; one now experiencing gentrification with the development of high rises. At seventeen years old, I was the youngest member of my household comprised of SFSU students, aged twenty-five to thirty-two. I reveled in my mature off-campus city lifestyle, away from the fogbound dorms. My rent, a mere $135 a month, was less than half of what it would cost to share an absurdly small room on campus with a same-aged student. And, as the younger "sibling" of my adult roommates, I was taken to parties, art shows in South-of-Market warehouses, and nightclubs.

Mass transit made the commute to school easy; I traveled through the Western Addition on the 24 Divisidero bus for Market Street and Castro, where shiny metal escalators descended underground into the Castro Street Muni station, allowing me to complete the second leg of my journey on the M train. In the late afternoons, as the fog rolled over Twin Peaks and I waited to board the bus for home, I would observe leather-clad men descending upon the local bars and restaurants under the cover of rainbow colored flags, an exciting, transformative scene.

I remained in loose contact with my family, distancing myself as best I could from our saga. I don't remember exactly how or when my brother came to live with my father. What I do remember is that my father had finally taken my mother to court to fight for custody of my brother and had won.

What happened to my mother after my brother moved to Pasadena is mostly a blur. I remember hearing about how she was staying in a hotel in downtown Los Angeles when she was robbed of a family inheritance, thousands of dollars in gold Krugerrands that she carried on her person in a small black purse. I also learned that Mom lived in hotels or short-term rentals in the San Fernando Valley. Before following John to Los Angeles, she had become rail thin, having pretty much stopped eating. Because of her appearance, he confided in me, she struggled to find someone who would rent her an apartment or even allow her to book a room in a hotel.

My brother's weekly visits with my mother were typically punctuated by her desperate pleas not to be left behind. When my father would arrive in his white economy Mazda GLC to pick up his son, Mom would wedge herself into the open car door, demanding that he allow her to come home with them. The three would then agonize for some time in the middle of the street before my father could persuade my mother to step out of the way and let him take John, leaving her standing there.

Perhaps this was around the time of "the nudie nightie incident," as my brother refers to it, when my mother was found wandering in a confused state around her Encino apartment building at night. After this, my brother recognized the need for my mother to get psychiatric help. At sixteen years old, John was too young to get the police involved, so he convinced my father to help him call 911 and have my mother declared a danger to herself and involuntarily committed. She was taken to UCLA Neuropsychiatric Hospital where she finally received proper treatment for a formerly undiagnosed mental illness.

After her release, with the help of cousins living on the Westside, she found an apartment in Beverly Hills. Continuing to struggle with no sense of place or direction, she routinely flew between Los Angeles, Texas, and New York, landing on her sisters for months at a time until finally, after she had lost her bags in the Dallas Airport, she collapsed. Catatonic, she was again involuntarily committed for several months. Upon release, she then went to live with her parents in Zimbabwe, where she finally stabilized.

"Your mother suffers from manic depression accompanied by the feature of paranoia," was more or less how my father explained it to me. The diagnosis served in some small way to contextualize the past. "Neurotic" had never done justice to my mother's symptoms: the bouts of senseless laughter, sleepless nights, paranoid accusations, disturbing hallucinations. However, I would not learn about the full scope of my mother's illness until I was twenty-four years old.

Miracle Baths

In the second year of college, I was lucky to find a part-time job to supplement my $450 monthly stipend sent to me by my father. Through a friend in my English class, Linda Landels, a returning student at thirty-three years old, I came to work for two Nebraskan transplants, women and romantic partners in their late twenties who had moved to San Francisco at the end of the 1970s to pursue the dream of an alternative lifestyle.

I booked appointments and folded towels at the first spa in the city to garner a reputation for its healing arts, as opposed to those known for sexual activity. A forerunner of the day spa, Miracle Baths was a vibrant place to work. Everyone bestowed great admiration upon the owners, Penny and Kathy. One blonde, the other raven-haired, they dazzled us all with their bohemian, thrift store know-how: the 1950s clutch purses, vintage cars, kitschy outfits, cowboy leather jackets. Endowed with Midwestern DIY decorating skills, shuttling between city and country homes—albeit modest ones—my first real employers, "lipstick lesbians" as they called themselves, struck me as model feminists. Women I dearly sought to emulate.

Unafraid of the rigors of work, for the first five years of their entrepreneurial adventure they toiled around the clock, six- or seven-days a week, twelve hours or more per day. The spa's rates were affordable, giving credence to the term "community sauna." Sadly, they did not invest in buying their property and would later lose out to a bigger, brasher gentrifying force, one capable of buying the building and replacing the spa with a store merchandizing unforgettably frivolous items like soap-on-a-rope. Even more dispiriting was the loss of life endured by the community when several of the staff members and close associations passed away—

Jerry, Jose, Marshall and Tommy, one after the other—from the scourge of a then-insufficiently researched and cruelly stigmatizing HIV virus and its virulent later stage of untreated symptoms, AIDS.

My mother is a witch

While my mother worked to piece her life back together, I bloomed precariously into young adulthood: traipsing about a picturesque, easily navigable city; studying poetry, philosophy, interdisciplinary arts; frequenting night clubs in the Tenderloin; and falling in love unexpectedly with a budding female poet while my mother continued her battle with an illness for which the treatment was rudimentary at best.

These were difficult, unhappy years during which I resisted my mother's presence in my life. She was still fairly manic. Her persistent calls, her alarming and indeterminate living situations, threatened the tenuous stability I had carved out for myself. I knew my mother would call me every day, several times, if she could. I knew how depressed I would become.

San Francisco State did not turn out to be the hotbed of social and political activism that it had been in the 1960s and 1970s. While I took women's studies classes from celebrities like Angela Davis, overall the atmosphere on campus after the election of Ronald Reagan was downbeat, with an ever-increasing crop of students interested in obtaining MBAs. For two years, I successfully dodged my mother. She never did get my phone number in that time. I moved so often then, keeping it from her was not exactly difficult.

In my third year, I remember being seated at my small black desk in the bay window of my Hayes Street apartment at my electric typewriter, reveling in the ecstatic California sunshine. This was my mother's typewriter I had somehow inherited, the Selectric with the missing "g."

"My mother is a witch," I banged out, in the midst of typing out a poem, when the phone rang. Having grown weary of my disappearing act, my brother had given her my phone number.

Hearing my mother's voice on the line, I knew then that I would always be her daughter. I knew I could no longer run away.

G-spot

I will never forget the glory and shame of working on that particular typewriter. Unable to afford a new one, or perhaps unwilling to spend my weekly part-time cash on something practical, painstakingly I wrote in all of the "g"s of my academic papers by hand. This took time. Only when my philosophy of science teacher made a cutting joke about my "g-spot" in reference to one of my frenetic-looking, hand-edited papers did I finally put some of my part-time earnings toward the purchase of another typewriter.

I still remember the poems I wrote, and the disorienting quality the hand drawn "g's" added to the work. One in particular stands out in my memory—"And it was running thin," a poem I wrote under the influence of the Language poets working in the Bay Area at that time: Carla Harryman, Barrett Watten, Leslie Scalapino, and Jim Hartz, the director of the Poetry Center at SFSU, to name a few. My allegiance to their work was immediate, mainly because a strict adherence to realism was anything but the point. I had space to claim the page for my own needs, to express the inexpressible through disjunctive and surrealist techniques. The writer who compelled me most, though, was Kathy Acker, a tough, satiric pop maven, whose intertextual collage techniques and recursive themes of an abandoning father and a hateful mother, appealed to my psychic wounds as well as to my preference for dank intellectual chaos. This writer was fucked up and unafraid of the fact, harnessing her erotic feminist heresy and taking it into uncharted territories.

Aside from Acker, the Language poets were a fairly hermetic group that held the commercially successful, arguably macho, narrative-based writing of the Beats in contempt. I found myself mutely adhering to the experimentation of the Language poets, while my poet girlfriend managed to breech the divide, making in-roads in both communities. It was not lost on me that the Language poets operated in a narrow tranche of experimentation that in some small measure reflected back my family's elite intellectual background.

Shortly after my mother's eerily timed phone call, we reunited. Again, the memory is mostly shrouded. Did she come to see me in San Francisco? Did I go to see her in New Jersey where she finally decided to settle after coming to terms with the loss of her son to college and the West Coast? I cannot say. I do remember that I took full advantage of our rekindled bond when I went to spend a long weekend in New York City with my best friend from SFSU, budding experimental filmmaker Mark Taylor. We stayed with Mark's cousin in the East Village, visiting art galleries, punk clubs like the Pyramid, and museums. His dewy-eyed cousin served us free margaritas at the East Village Mexican restaurant where she waitressed. We hardly slept, and visited another friend, Jonathon Rosen, an illustrator whose ability to make a living at his art impressed me to no end.

Soon Mark and I ran out of money, so I quickly organized a meeting with my mother in the hopes of borrowing some more. She took us for a steak dinner at a restaurant in the World Trade Center. At one point she dumped out the contents of her purse, with its heavy collection of coins, on a marble counter in the lobby in order to find subway fare. The time it took for her to release the purse's contents was stupefying. Glittering coins by the handful clattered loudly onto the long marble counter as my friend laughed brightly, utterly charmed by my mother's eccentricities. A side effect of the medication she was on, my mother struggled with the adroit use of her hands. I adored Mark all the more for his ability to find humor where I could only find despair. Was it $100 or $200 that she loaned me? I cannot recall.

Whatever the amount, I recall it endowing me with a feeling of ease and profligacy that I relished on that short, glorious visit. After this, I came to appreciate my mother's generosity on more than one occasion. She never required that I pay her back, even though she subsisted on a limited alimony, and later, social security payments, both of which afforded her little more than the ability to pay her rent and purchase the expensive pharmaceuticals her disease demanded, despite being insured.

By the end of my years at SFSU, my mother and I had crossed over from a terrible time into a markedly better one.

1984–2011

Even so, the time we spent together was strictly regulated. As the recipient of the nurture and assistance of numerous second-wave feminists, I declined my mother's attentions in favor of so many glorious others. In college, there were the women associated with Miracle Baths; later on in Los Angeles, a woman who ran a Pilates studio long before it became a popular exercise was determined to see me become more agile and fit after years of unhealthy smoking and angsty brooding.

I always felt grateful to these self-sufficient women who willingly befriended and mentored me. That they had taken the time to assert their independence, running businesses that took the majority of their waking days made these "unchilded women," in the words of Adrienne Rich, my feminist heroes. I was aware that the work it took to raise children properly was a parent's necessary sacrifice, something my mother did not care to or was unable to do. But a capitalist system that did not provide reasonable daycare left women of this generation few choices as they carved out their identities.

Out of filial duty, I would see my mother once a year. Visiting her in New Jersey at first until this became too much for me, for a variety of reasons. Top of the list: my distress in seeing my mother living far below the economic station of my father, alone in a small, one-bedroom apartment with little comfort or grace. Chatham, New Jersey, where she finally ended up after years of living in a red brick apartment she would sarcastically deride (*Time to go back to the hovel*), had too much in common with the provincial Berkeley Heights of my youth, with its massive trees and narrow winding roads, a town that symbolized for me endless psychic despair.

Mom, I would say over the telephone from Los Angeles, where I was making my living as an adjunct professor, *I can't visit. I'll get depressed.*

I understand, darling, she would routinely respond, her voice softened now by the years. *Don't come.*

Uncomplainingly, she would make the long journey by air to visit me in California. This was never easy for my mother. She suffered from varying degrees of *alogia*, an inability to make decisions. If a relative invited her to Passover and she had to travel by train, she would suffer over her decision to go for weeks in advance, changing her mind often.

Go, Mom, I would insist, knowing how much of her time was spent alone. A short weekend visit with family would provide her a much-needed break from the endless monotony of living alone without meaningful work or nearby family.

During college I had not given much thought to making money. After a number of half-hearted attempts at working in an administrative role for corporate America or as a "girl Friday" for this or that Hollywood charlatan, I found myself working at the *L.A. Weekly*, founded in 1978 by Jay Levin. It was here that renowned writers and critics made impressive contributions to the literature of Los Angeles; among them, Steve Erickson, the film critic and cult fiction writer, and Jonathan Gold, Pulitzer Prize winning popular food critic. This independent weekly newsprint tabloid was widely known for its tawdry glut of phone-sex ads juxtaposed with its hard-hitting investigative news articles, strong arts criticism, and comprehensive calendar of arts and music events. This was the one and only publication in Los Angeles, with the exception perhaps of Larry Flynt's *Hustler*, where a progressive young writer might get her start.

After three years of working for the permissive, alternative women of Miracle Baths, where prayer circles were not an uncommon reaction to adversity, I was hardly cut out to work anywhere that smacked of corporate routine. My entry-level messenger job at the *L.A. Weekly* had all the glamorous appeal you might expect. I spent exasperatingly long periods of time alone in my aged Toyota Corolla, manual windows cranked down, inhaling a gross number of Marlboro Light cigarettes in the smog-tainted heat, tracking down advertising money from small businesses in Hollywood and the Westside, and when especially unlucky, the gridded Valley, where I felt adrift on the long, lonesome roadways. Because advertisers, typically small business owners, were loath to pay their bills, picking up checks was essential. Hired at $6.50 an hour plus mileage (where the bulk of our real earnings came from, and which our tender-hearted rocker boss, Luke, allowed us to inflate at the end of the week), I could afford little in the way of anything, really, subsisting on a steady diet of canned Rosarito refried beans and a steady stream of cigarettes.

As far as thrifting went, I relied heavily on the meager holdings of a $5 clothing store located in a stucco strip mall at the busy Vermont/Hollywood intersection. This consisted mainly of patterned mini-skirts and brightly colored Lycra tank tops. For footwear I succumbed to the ubiquitously worn cowboy boots of the Exene Cervenka-driven 1980s. My long brown hair was dyed a shocking pink, the result of a catastrophic professional hair-dying incident—a fantastic color that secretly repulsed me.

The upside of this unskilled job, a position held almost exclusively by male rockers of the Guns N' Roses variety—with the exception of one petite raven-haired girlfriend of an up-and-coming rock star, who stopped coming to work the moment her makeup purchases were satisfied—was that I had the ear of talented editors who allowed me to sidestep the unpaid intern process and be paid for my writing, the rate then being about ten cents a word. Writing short articles for the paper, I was schooled in the basics of journalism.

Again, I found a friend and *mother*, or mentor, in a former dancer and artist named Marilyn Amaral. Marilyn worked in paste-up with her "hag sisters" Donita Sparks of all-girl punk band L7 and dreadlock-sporting Pollyanne. A cousin of Miles Davis, the daughter of a renowned Tuskegee airman and former *Solid Gold* dancer and La MaMa performer, Marilyn was statuesque, brilliant and unspeakably beautiful, determined to live a life of great highs and lows. Having endured the regular beatings of her would-be-actor husband of ten years who suffered from manic depression, she eventually separated from him to make a life of her own as a makeup artist. No matter what challenge confronted me—rent troubles, boyfriend torments, editorial tiffs—I had a kind and charming confidante in Marilyn.

Driving the streets of Los Angeles, long before Waze, I learned the best routes to take at all times of day, another plus, until the low-paying and mind-numbing job grew unbearable. Soon a hastily landed career in door-to-door political fundraising would become my mainstay.

824 ½ Maltman Avenue

Shortly after moving to Los Angeles in 1987, I inherited from a friend a large studio apartment in Silver Lake. Less than $500 a month and nestled at the top of a hill, the stucco 1920s apartment, with windows filled with the swooning branches of a large pepper tree, was located at Maltman Avenue and Marathon Boulevard, adjacent to the Bellevue Recreation Center and Park, where gang activity was still fairly common. For years, I convinced myself that the loud nighttime crackling sounds were fireworks. Often in summer, I would leave the front door of the cottage open, allowing the fragrant Los Angeles night air to fill the two-room apartment. It was here that I discovered my mother's proper diagnosis. I imagine it was my brother who informed me.

That my mother's diagnosis was paranoid schizophrenia and not manic depression filled me with a sinking despair. I spent the following week, with my live-in boyfriend helpfully away in San Francisco, at the library in downtown Los Angeles acquainting myself with the illness. But there were far fewer books on the topic than there are today.

The scientific books were for me, at the time, perplexing and uninteresting, and soon I limited myself to the literature of psychoanalysis. This left me in the backyard of R.D. Laing, famous for spearheading the anti-psychiatry movement, whose work in at least some small measure linked schizophrenia with environmental factors such as poor parenting. Was his theory correct? It didn't feel all that unreasonable to blame my mother's parents for her troubles: a distant, work-obsessed father and a mother who had no trouble sending her fleet of daughters thousands of miles away from Zimbabwe to be schooled in England while she catered to her husband's endless ambitions, seemed troubling to me, and definitely outside a modern conception of family, one where children are prized beyond words.

It felt suitable to blame someone. In the face of tragedy, it is compelling to attempt to root out a single social or human cause. I was not immune from scapegoating. Blaming my mother's parents for their daughter's mental state came easy. For years, I had already suspected that my mother's misery was in some way a karmic debt for having participated in a colonial system that cruelly subjugated African people on their own continent. Gender inequality in her parental home as well as a host of other social prohibitions also came into the picture. After all, childrearing and housework hardly commanded my mother's attention. The daughter of an acclaimed doctor and married to a world-class scientist, she was under an insubordinate pressure to make something of herself. This was at the root of her affliction. This was the story I told myself. Her father's routine boasts only made things worse.

Now I could add poor parenting to my list of causes for her illness.

But then why didn't I suffer from schizophrenia? If poor parenting were to blame, wouldn't I also suffer from the same illness? My parents ridiculed my choices, derided my need for love, and were often too busy with their respective careers to pay close attention to me or to my brother. My mother routinely insulted me, pulled my hair, and slapped me; commonly accused me of all kinds of wild, inappropriate behaviors, most often of being a prostitute.

Why then was I not suffering from paranoid delusions like my mother? Why was I not anhedonic most of the time, with no hobbies or interests outside of work?

I became suspicious of this and just about every other psychoanalytic basis of her disease.

Hereditary aspect

The book I gleaned the most from, titled something like *Everything You Wanted to Know About Schizophrenia But Were Afraid to Ask*, with a self-help cover and sized like a VHS videotape, was written by a journalist, whose son had been diagnosed with this chronic illness. Thankfully this book provided me with a continuum on which to place the radical ideas of R.D. Laing. Notable for maintaining the notion that schizophrenia was "an idea and not a fact," the vanguard psychiatrist was more willing to treat the whole person suffering from schizophrenia than other psychiatrists who were influenced primarily by genetic and biological definitions. The idea this journalist espoused after collating a long history of treatment on this disease was even more, a holistic one. In her book, she dissected and summarized the various approaches to curing or alleviating the primary symptoms of the illness. From neurobiology to nutrition to talk therapy, she deemed all approaches essential in seeking a solution, and her thesis struck me as both balanced and clarifying. She did not assign one root cause for the illness nor create a hierarchy for the types of cures, so I had faith in her approach. A mother herself, she knew better than to assign herself blame for her son's illness. Through her experience of caring for her son, she could see how easy it was for others to blame the family; and how useless the casting of blame was in the pursuit of a cure.

Most distressing to me then was the hereditary aspect of the disease. I had not considered this consciously before, though I must have had some sense of its inevitability. As a first-degree relative, according to the literature, I would have a seventeen percent chance of inheriting the illness. In the case of my children, second-degree relatives, the chances would be as high as thirty-three percent.[9] This was disturbing news, and I immediately confronted my father by telephone about the omission.

"Why didn't you tell me the truth? Schizophrenia is hereditary. My children could have a thirty-three percent chance of inheriting this illness."

"Try not to worry, Claire," my scientist father advised in his typical low-key fashion. "You have my genes."

---

9 Today, while the chance for inheriting this disease is the same for a first-degree relative, in the case of a second-degree relative, the chance has been lowered to five percent.

New Providence, New Jersey, 1988

No sooner than I learned the truth, my mother suffered a relapse. Perhaps she had forgotten to take her medication. Or she decided not to take it at the prompting of "an inner voice." It was many years before she was able to embrace the full reality of her illness. It is also possible that at the time she merely accepted her doctor's suggestion that she reduce the dose of medication she was taking. Whatever the reason, my mother was experiencing a bout of psychosis. My brother was away on school-related business, so it was my turn to intervene during a long weekend with her in New Jersey.

Her manner on the phone had been erratic, delusional. When I arrived, she was still functioning, shuffling around her dim, one-bedroom apartment, adhering to domestic duties such as laundry. She had made a bed for me from the pullout sofa.

While I had been called in to help, I found out almost immediately that I was utterly useless. As my mother stormed about, espousing her fears, I sank into a paralyzing torpor on the makeshift bed. I began to question my sense of the situation. Was she really ill? So ill that she needed to be hospitalized? Would a hospitalization even help? I couldn't be sure, and cleaved to my spot on the sofa, watching as my mother sorted through her clothes, getting ready to confront the dank basement to do her laundry.

Periodically, she would stand hypnotically before the drawn curtains of her living room windows and repeat in a fear-struck voice, *I'm the only one here. Tomorrow they are coming to demolish the place.*

I was pained by these words. They seemed more symbolic than anything else. My mother had been abandoned to live alone in New Jersey, while the rest of us, in at least some small part, thrived in California. Yes, she was alone here. And yes, the experience of schizophrenia, of the inexplicable neurological disruption, must have paralleled this feeling of being alone, on the verge of being dismantled by outside forces.

Whenever my mother spoke like this I grew more despondent, more ashamed of my inability to make her life more tolerable. Only when the weekend came to a close and I returned to California, did my mother receive the care she rightly deserved. No longer willing to bear the heavy weight of her psychosis alone, she drove herself to a nearby hospital to seek out treatment. Back then, she was able to recover in a relatively short length of time.

A vacation with Mom

After her recovery, I took my mother with me on a short weekend trip to Rosarito Beach in Baja, Mexico. This spot, where Hollywood stars once vacationed during Prohibition, boasted an old-fashioned Mission-style hotel with a swimming pool and a somewhat disappointing oil-streaked beach. It was picturesque if you didn't leave the hotel, and it was what I could afford. A college friend joined us.

At twenty-four years old, I wasn't much of a daughter, struggling with the discomfort I felt toward my mother's obvious afflictions: the muscle rigidity, dystonia, and tardive dyskinesia (TD), all side effects of the first-generation anti-psychotic, Haldol. TD involved facial tics and involuntary twisting of her fingers, but she did not suffer from the restlessness so many patients complained about.

Haldol, the standard treatment then or "good ole vitamin H" as some called it, was one of the first medications used in the treatment of schizophrenia. According to the National Alliance on Mental Illness, this antipsychotic works as an inverse agonist of dopamine to rebalance "emotion and lower cognitive function in order to improve thinking, mood, and behavior." The drug has some ability to ameliorate primary symptoms of schizophrenia such as hallucinations, delusions, and disordered thinking, but mostly fails to treat the secondary features of her illness, namely the depression, lack of affect, and poverty of feeling.

Throughout the trip I recall my former college roommate Mara and me trying to spend time on our own, in the gardens and on the sunny porches of the property, with my mother working to trail along, her purse strapped anxiously to her side. She was terrified of it being stolen or lost, and her exaggerated fear caused me great distress. With perhaps a slippery sense of reality, my mother was often worried and would announce her fears on a continual basis. Because her life had narrowed so significantly, conversation often felt difficult and forced. It would be many years before I would deign to take her with me on another vacation, and even then it was for the shortest time imaginable.

While my father remained distant, involved with his work and the responsibilities of a second family, my mother could find comfort only through speaking to her children. For years, it was my mother's habit to call both my brother and me several times a day. She would leave messages on our answering machines at first and then continue to call. I rarely answered her calls, or when I did, I would lie and tell her I was headed out, and could speak for just a moment. I afforded her little of my time or energy. Not a day would pass without considering how I had abandoned my mother to an unthinkable loneliness. Ashamed at not making a place for her in my life, I felt routinely submerged in despair. I could not fathom how to help her make a new life for herself. She could not afford to live in California with the rest of us and found it hard to make friends. Sometimes Mom spoke of a woman down the hall with whom she would occasionally have tea, though I could hardly imagine my driven, no-nonsense mother deriving much pleasure from idle chitchat.

Annoyed perhaps that he had to provide my mother with an income, whenever I spoke to my father on the topic of her wellbeing, he would invariably respond that she get a job. For whatever reason, he could not comprehend how difficult it was for her to perform the simplest tasks. She struggled with driving, with the adroit use of her hands, and worried ceaselessly over the tiniest of decisions. Bagging groceries at the local supermarket? Working as a clerk at the local library? I could never envision what it would be, this job that he suggested she get.

5

zinza

Filial duties

On July 12, 1985, at seventy-three years old, Grandpa Mike
died of heart failure while performing his rounds at the
Harare Central Hospital. He had known for some time that
he was dying. After my mother had been committed at UCLA,
he had come to realize that her illness was a chronic one and
that she would always be in need of care. Addressing John
over the phone, he openly counseled my fifteen-year-old
brother on his filial duties.

"When I die, it will be your responsibility to take care of
your mother."

More than a little stunned, John assented to his distant
grandfather's instruction and ministered to my mother's
copious legal and medical needs, almost exhaustively, for the
next twenty-eight years.

More dreams

Despite not being able to fully understand my mother's
illness, I was determined not to lose sight of her heritage.
At twenty-three and while living in Los Angeles, I started
dreaming of my deceased grandfather. In my dream, he
inexplicably became a close family member to the Steinberg
daughters, three dark-haired Jewish sisters with whom I
mildly associated while taking Body Weather Laboratory
Workshop classes from avant-garde dancers Melinda Ring

and Roxanne Steinberg at LACE,[10] located near the L.A. river in a converted brick warehouse. During these three-hour intensives I became familiar with the rigors of Japanese Butoh, which Ring and Steinberg learned while training with Min Tanaka in Japan on his Body Workshop butoh farm. The three-hour classes were both highly demanding and deeply revelatory—from the hour of mind/body exercises (MB) followed by deep partner stretches, to the improvisational and sensory work.

In my dream, I would approach my grandfather hoping to connect, only to discover he had no idea who I was. The Steinbergs were clearly stand-ins for my mother and her sisters. It occurred to me then that I knew very little about my mother's family. I had rejected offers to visit my grandparents as a child, and my mother had no interest in returning to her birth country. An outsider to my own family in the dream, I decided I needed to visit Zimbabwe and my grandmother, who lived on her own in Harare in what had been my mother's childhood home until she was sent to boarding school in England. I wrote to my grandmother and asked her to send me a ticket. A round trip ticket to Zimbabwe in 1990 was about as costly then as it is now: $2,000. I made enough money to pay for these Saturday workshops and not much more.

No one in my family seemed eager for me to make this trip. Despite that, I deemed my grandfather's overt dismissal of me in favor of the Steinbergs, however metaphorical, too much to bear. Only when I made the arrangements did the dreams of familial estrangement end.

---

10 Los Angeles Contemporary Exhibitions (LACE) is an experimental arts organization founded in 1978 with an activist, community-oriented vision for art as an agent of social change.

After Zimbabwe gained independence, in order to prevent a
tragic, economic collapse of the new state, the predominately
white citizens who had benefited from the gross inequities
of colonialism were forbidden from taking their money
out of the country. As I had little money of my own, my
grandmother and I would exchange letters for several
months before she was able to secure the funds for me to buy
the costly ticket via relatives in South Africa.

My grandmother's letters were written on the same
self-sealing blue airmail paper that she had used for as long
as I could remember when writing to her three daughters
living in the U.S. These international letters, filled with
breezy accounts of daily life, were so superficial that my
mother had stopped opening them long ago, leaving them
to pile up throughout the house. After reading a few, I
could understand why. Rote and unemotional, they seemed
more like diary entries than heartfelt communication from
mother to daughter.

Harare, Zimbabwe

Except for the furniture, everything in my grandmother's
thatched-roof stucco house had been a gift. On my first
evening in the capital city of Zimbabwe, I was shown
through the modest one-story 1920s home, and made privy
to the history behind each object hanging on the walls
or propped up on shelves. Impressive African landscape

paintings; African sculptures of various sizes and shapes, the most notable being the Shona soapstone works—curved abstractions in green or black; the traditional ritualistic objects of the Shona religious culture such as the mbiria, drums, the woven baskets, and the divining bones of the witch doctor—the *hakata*. In my grandfather's small study with metal case windows looking onto overgrown waxy green plants, were rows and rows of books. These included mostly medical books, a few classic British and South African novels, and dozens of copies of the thirty-two books he had authored.

Early in his career he wrote a book called *The Sick African*, which dispensed useful information on the treatment of tropical diseases from a clinical medical point of view, emphasizing the difference between Bantu and Western attitudes toward disease. As it was described by Negley Farson of the Oxford Academic in 1946:

> It is that kind of book; a handbook destined to be upon the table of doctors, nuns, priests, medical-missionaries, colonial administrators, in fact, every white man and woman working in Equatorial Africa, who has to treat the sick African. And it is a book that would be of great value to the average Britisher, if you could only get people at home to read it; it might shock them out of their dangerous indifference about the *obligations* of the British Empire.[11]

Farson goes on to note the shocking nature of the photographs in particular: "These sores, distortions, and gruesome disfigurements of the human body speak of agonies never meant for man to bear." The concerns my

---

11 Farson, Negley. "The Sick African: A Clinical Study." *OUP Academic*, Oxford University Press, Volume 45, Issue 178, 1 Jan. 1946. Web.

grandfather expressed in this book took note of the fact that Africans suffered more profoundly from tropical diseases than their white or European counterparts, who were less susceptible. As Africans performed all of the "heavy work," this was of particular concern. Most emphatically, in the chapter titled "The Life and Outlook of the Native," the mistrust of native people toward white Western medicine was explored. While medical observation makes up the bulk of this work—for example, the interpretation of symptoms that are seemingly unrelated to systemic tropical diseases— some of the work was criticized and in subsequent editions revised. The colonial interpretation of African rituals and traditions was troubling, including sections about the medical practices of the witch doctor. This is evidenced by the title, which today appears nothing short of pejorative.

Other books written by my grandfather focused on the customs and the religious and ritualistic practices of the Shona or Mashona, the majority tribe in Zimbabwe. The inception of this research and writing was a friendship between Mike and a *n'anga* who had walked three days to the hospital where my grandfather practiced medicine, seeking treatment. My grandfather admired the tribe's strong religious and moral codes, gained admittance to many ritualistic practices, and began a process of recording his findings. Not schooled in ethnography, and not of African descent, these works were met with criticism on both sides of the colonial divide. Works that include photographs of people whose ritualistic lifestyle is almost entirely abandoned today.

In one such book, *Shona Ritual*, printed in 1959, there are multiple photographs of a female spirit medium becoming possessed by the spirit of *Chaminuka* in one of main huts, or *banya*, during a ceremony to ask for rain. Tribal tutelary spirits are named and delineated. The role and practices of the *n'anga*, healer and diviner, are explained and recorded along with the prominent position of the *mudzimu*, the ancestral spirit or spirit elder.

N'anga

My grandmother, at seventy-six years old, was petite and silver haired and still able to get about fairly well considering recent brushes with colon cancer and hip surgery. She spent her days writing in a journal or visiting with friends within the rambling, yet modestly appointed home set within an abundance of tropical plants and trees. Her house servants, Jane and Artilla, her driver and cook respectively, were housed somewhat shamefully in the small partitioned garage with their families. Her Jack Russell terrier, Littley, was her constant companion, nipping at her heels, or perched adoringly on her lap.

There was rarely a dull moment in her home. Over the course of my first week there, I discovered it was not uncommon for visitors to drop by unannounced at all hours of the day. Almost always they came bearing baked goods, delicious Jewish meals, or special gifts of books or medical publications. The affection they held for my grandmother was of a familial kind. It was astonishing really. A woman who, at best, had been a distant figure in my mother's life, was at the center of a large community of friends. Despite her conservative colonial-infected views on race and gender, she was exceptionally good company. Respectful. Generous. Each week, perfectly aware of my cash-strapped state, she would go to the supply store with Jane, and bring me back a carton of Zimbabwe cigarettes, a product of the thriving tobacco industry in this country at that time. No other relative would have indulged this accursed habit of mine.

Only when I grew restless with the daily routine of accompanying her on errands or taking walks around the city did I begin to discover another side of my grandmother. The restrictions were painfully familiar. After hearing beguiling stories of the witch doctors, the *n'anga* with whom my grandfather had worked for years exchanging information about the healing arts, I grew curious to meet one of these former associates who had conferred upon him an honorary membership into their practices. As my grandmother told the story: on the anniversary of my grandfather's death for three consecutive years, ten or so witch doctors would travel for miles from rural areas to her home to honor him in a drum ceremony and summon his spirit.

"They always arrived on the wrong date, but I never told them," she confided. When I suggested that I meet some of these men whose traditions were vastly different from my own, her cut and dry answer was, "You can't. They are all dead."

When it came to social prohibitions, I knew just how stubborn my mother's family could be. My grandmother didn't feel it would be proper that I meet these men, and so, for whatever reason, I was forbidden.

Equally stubborn, I would not be sidetracked. I had discovered something out of the ordinary: a bona fide relationship to a mystical domain discredited by European post-Enlightenment culture. A neophyte Pagan, I was determined to open that door.

One-party rule

It had been my intent when traveling in Zimbabwe to exercise my newfound journalism skills. However, the country was notoriously unfriendly to journalists. Under the autocratic one-party rule of President Robert Mugabe, the leader of the ZANU-PF (Zimbabwe African National Union – Patriotic Front) and a man known for military heroism battling Ian Smith and the English forces of colonialism, Zimbabwe suffered from rampant corruption among government officials. Everything was bought and sold on the black market, including foreign currency. Food was scarce. The majority of citizens scraped by on mealie meal for sustenance, ground corn boiled and patted into mild-tasting, sticky balls. If lucky, they might add to their meal a few ounces of steamed vegetable—okra, as I recall— or a small helping of meat or fish. For obscure reasons, the one and only building project on the perimeter of Harare, a luxury hotel, was on permanent hold due to a cement scarcity. There were no car parts. The Lancaster House rule, a decree that had been signed during independence which allowed white land owners to keep their land, was due to end, and the white farmers were terrified at the prospect of losing their land. What would Mugabe do?

Before arriving in Harare, I consulted *The Lonely Planet* guide to Zimbabwe, the bohemian backpackers's handbook for travel. On the topic of journalism, it was suggested that I declare my status as a journalist right off the bat rather then be denied interviews from government officials and members of NGOs later on. Putting my faith in this tome of low-cost global travel, having already put it to good use a few years before when climbing the Inca Trail to Machu Picchu, I made a terrible mistake. Arriving in Zimbabwe, I declared my visiting status on the inflight handout to be work-related even though I was primarily in Africa to visit my grandmother, ticking off the box for journalism. At customs I was told that my visa of three months would not be granted until I met with a certain government official to discuss my work in the country as a journalist.

Friends of the Earth

I could not believe my bad luck. The one time I acted in accordance with the rules, I was in trouble. A few days after I arrived, I appeared at the government building in downtown Harare for a meeting with the media official in a bare tiled room with the aged furnishings of a metal desk and a few wooden chairs. The no-nonsense African woman's authoritarian demeanor produced in me the desired effect—an impending sense of doom. I could not be sent back to America, not after all it took to get here. I pulled out all the stops. I mentioned that my grandfather had been the official doctor to President Mugabe's mother, and that the President himself had spoken at my grandfather's funeral. I explained that I had mistakenly ticked the wrong box. My sole purpose in visiting Zimbabwe was personal, I averred—to spend time with my grandmother. I was a journalist writing about arts-related events in America. I was not an international reporter. This was more or less the case.

Even so, I had the hope of investigating environmental matters, having persuaded Jay Levin, the founder and President of the *L.A. Weekly* to allow me to do research for a special issue of the paper related to global warming and its implications for the world. I had a special interest in conservation efforts. It seemed to me, after doing research in San Francisco in the small library of the nonprofit organization Friends of the Earth, first founded in 1969 as an antinuclear group, that global warming was the most pressing issue of my time. Yet it registered not a wit with capitalist American society—the consumerist world kept turning in the same unsustainable direction. Somehow, I succeeded in persuading the official in charge of my case to let me go, my family background having bought me some breathing room. I was clearly not there to blow the whistle on Mugabe's extreme and violent practices against his own people.

Only later did my self-anointed role as a journalist pay off. Shortly after my grandmother had insisted I would not be able to meet with any *n'anga* associates of my grandfather, I came upon an article in the daily *Herald* about the Association of the Zimbabwe Spirit Mediums (the AZSM) who were working to reforest Zimbabwe. The AZSM was led by Dr. Daneel, a white professor in the southeastern town of Masvingo. The main purpose of this group was to remedy local environmental degradation attributed to colonization: deforestation and the ensuing soil erosion. Through meeting with *mudzimu*, these spirit mediums, I would satisfy my twinned interests of environmental redress and non-traditional mystical practices. I would travel to Bulawayo on my own, engaging in my own way with my grandfather's legacy.

I called the association the following day.

"Is Dr. Daneel there?"

"He is away on business. I am his associate. How may I help you?"

I explained my position as an American journalist interested in both environmental activism and traditional Shona culture.

"Dr. Daneel is away for the next two weeks, but you are welcome to come here," the young male associate said, responding to my request to interview the head of the organization. I was then informed about the organization's goal to plant trees in an effort to fight desertification, a direct result of colonial farming practices and a problem that, according to the Washington D.C.-based NGO World Watch, would only intensify with global warming.

My grandmother had absolutely no intention of letting me travel a journey of this distance on a bus alone. I was a young woman. What would my mother think? Desperate to find me companionship for such a trip, my grandmother began to invite all sorts of people over for tea. Friends of all ages and backgrounds flowed through the house, but these associations, while warm, were loose at best. A musicologist, an urban planner, and a married doctor-couple, whose findings on HIV were denied by the current government, were all invited over to meet me. But no one seemed interested in the friendship my grandmother had hoped would buffer me from solo adventures. So I persevered. When I discovered that Professor Daneel was away for several weeks on a research project I was crushed at first, but then immediately buoyed when it was suggested I could stay at the professor's house, the headquarters for the Association, and I was assured that I would be able to meet spirit mediums working on conservation issues. I was thrilled. My grandmother, however, still held to her position.

Transportation

While I billed myself as the great independent, I sorely lacked the funds to support my endeavors or initiatives. Visiting my grandmother was no exception. After three weeks in Zimbabwe, I was almost out of money. I was certainly not in a position to afford the ticket for a weekend bus trip of over one hundred miles, let alone sleeping accommodations over a long weekend. Granny would have to foot the bill. We were at loggerheads for some time. Becoming forlorn, I retreated to my room, despairing of my position. This had a discernible effect on my grandmother, who suddenly relented. I could take the bus.

In a week's time, I took off for Masvingo on public transportation. White people never took public transit. It was unthinkable, and certain rumors about its miseries abounded. "Didn't your bum hurt?" Amanda, an urban planner and friend of my grandmother's had asked after I returned. This was shocking, not just because I couldn't imagine a type of bus seat that would actually make my butt ache, but also because Amanda was not your traditional white, postcolonial elitist. She didn't expound hatred toward the new government or African rule. She wore a nose ring and spent her days overseeing investment in much-needed plumbing within "underdeveloped" rural areas. Endowed with great physical beauty and charisma, she was at the center of an ecstatic, underground multi-racial lesbian community in the capital city. It was a strange reaction— one that implied no one she cared to speak to had ever taken the bus, any bus, for any length of time.

Masvingo

During my first evening in the professor's home, his African associates welcomed me by discussing many topics openly. In the screened-off sun porch, as pink geckos climbed the slickly painted kitchen walls, we sat gathered about on the modest worn furniture, where I first asked about the spirit medium's role in traditional rituals. The role of the *mantonjeni*, the ancestral spirits that might come to possess you, was to inform the community of special concerns that would need to be addressed. Often this was how it worked: if a spirit had a grievance, the family would be required to give something particular to this spirit.

For example, it was explained to me that the spirit of a small child had entered one of the researcher's aunts. I learned that this particular child died early, after the related father had abandoned his many wives and children because his cattle were killed and he had become impoverished. The child was never given the chance to grow up, so this spirit asked for the aunt to be married and to have a child for the spirit.

"How did you know that your aunt was possessed by the spirit?" I asked.

"The child spirit entered the aunt, and she would crawl around like a baby when she was possessed."

The spirit spoke through her to the family and their spirit medium. It was perfectly acceptable, and the married couple was not afraid. Impressed by their willingness to share the precepts of a lifestyle so different from my own, I asked about race relations.

"Why are native Zimbabweans so comfortable with whites? ... Why aren't you angrier?" I asked in light of the brutal colonial practices that had pitted tribe against tribe, providing colonists with the rationale for having stolen the land and livelihood from the majority of these native people, largely subsistence farmers.

"It is not us who do not want to get along," Robert, the older of the two young male researchers confided, handsome and gleaming in his white cotton shirt. "The whites are the ones who like to keep separate from us." The lack of rancor in this young man's answer was striking.

A month later, I would travel for weeks alone in the most northern parts of Zimbabwe, where the Tonga people were the last to give up their traditions. In early 1990, despite the fact that the promised distribution of land had not worked out in the favor of the native African population and economic opportunity was being withheld from its citizenry by the corrupt ZANU-PF government, on this two-week sojourn and throughout my stay, I was struck by the generosity of almost everyone I met.

"Can I meet a spirit medium?" I asked at the end of the evening. My request was immediately granted with one caveat. "To get there, we will have to ride bicycles for several hours."

The next day Robert and I would ride bicycles for six hours along the well-traveled red clay paths of the grassy low savanna to the nearby Kyle National Park. It was the wet season in Zimbabwe, and the temperatures were mild, in the low eighties. Dotting the landscape under vast blue skies stood massive baobab trees with their sparse top-heavy branches resembling roots, made all the more dazzling by a panorama of very low white clouds. After a short visit to the historic Great Zimbabwe Ruins, the granite-walled enclave that had been home to the traditional cattle-herding people, the most impressive sub-Saharan ruins of their kind, we arrived at the spirit medium's home in the far eastern corner of the park with its rocky hills and vast grassland.

Spirit mediums played an important role in traditional Shona society. As experts, like elders or chiefs, they are responsible for safe guarding the traditional rituals in which ancestral spirits are evoked. The traditional *masvikiro* are capable of making oracular pronouncements and ensure a vital link between *mudzimu*, ancestral spirits, and the living. Struggles to elevate the importance of their role and gain legitimacy among the new establishment Africans post-independence are not uncommon. The AZSM had been organized in the 1980s under the auspices of the larger umbrella organization, AZTREC (Association of Zimbabwean Traditional Ecologists) in order to persuade the new government to recognize the needs and concerns of the rural traditional tribal members in their quest for environmental reform. During the revolution, their role was indisputably important as reported in the carefully researched book *Guns and Rain* by David Lan. The history of the Zimbabwe African National Liberation Army of which Robert Mugabe was a leader includes stories of tactical successes that were won based on the oracular predictions of the enemy's movements, those of the armies of Ian Smith.

The young researcher who had accompanied me on the bicycle ride served as translator. Seated on the floor of the spirit medium's traditional mud and thatched roof hut, I explained how that after dreaming of my dead grandfather I had come to Zimbabwe. The glittering-eyed spirit medium in the subdued simple shift and single copper bracelet smiled, relaying to me that I had *zinza*, a spiritual lineage. If I had dreamt of him, his spirit, or *sekura*, had come to me, and I was walking in his footsteps. I liked the sound of this. She then asked if people in our country performed a similar role to hers in Zimbabwe. I could only think of people who read tarot cards.

"Like the *n'anga* uses carved bones (*hakata*) to divine the future, there are people whose job it is to use cards with images to tell the future and solve problems," I told her. I had no trouble believing in the ancestral spirits however ambivalent I felt about my own.

"Have you visited your grandfather's grave?" the medium asked me, tucking a leg under the other where she sat before me on the dirt floor.

"No," I answered flatly. Having never participated in Jewish rituals, it had not occurred to me to do so.

Moved by the medium's question, when I returned to Harare, I asked my grandmother to take me to Grandpa's burial site. Accompanied by her terrier Littley, my grandmother and I journeyed in her 1960s four-door blue sedan with her driver and housekeeper, Jane, to the burial grounds and Ashkenazi Jewish temple, Warren Hills, modeled on the then-British moderate version of Orthodox Judaism. After we had shown our respects at my grandfather's grave, placing upon it flat stones in a Talmudic bid to help the "spirit stay put," Granny Esther recounted the story of her husband's burial four and a half years previous, including the details of the many notable people who had been present, like President Robert Mugabe, who came to pay his respects to his mother's doctor.

After this, Granny directed me to the outer reaches of the graveyard and a galvanized metal link fence behind which were several unmarked graves of those women who had been forbidden burial in the cemetery as they had married non-Jews. She didn't know these women personally but she "liked to visit them," she told me, reaching through the diagonal holes of the galvanized fence to place stones on their solemn graves. I did not take kindly to the treatment of these women or the strict exclusion of non-Jews advocated by traditional Jewish religion. Matters were made worse when I learned that men and women were prohibited from sitting together inside the synagogue. Apparently Judaism did not award women the same privileges as men, providing me a clear window into my mother's rejection of her father's orthodoxy.

During the three months that I stayed with my grandmother, I came to know something more about my grandfather beyond his restless need to discuss his work and the palpable tension I had witnessed between he and my mother. At the Harare Hospital, I was greeted by the head nurse dressed in white, stiff garments.

"I hope you will come to love all of us, both black and white equally, the same way your grandfather did with no prejudice," she remarked forthrightly as she took me between the various rooms of the two-story building. From her, I learned that my grandfather had pushed to desegregate the hospital so that those native to this country, and oppressed by colonial rule, could become versed in the practice of Western medicine.

The hospital was in a beleaguered state by American standards. Thin and drawn-looking patients, mostly male, lay upon stained mattresses insufficiently covered by torn, blood-soaked sheets. At 2 p.m. on Tuesdays, my grandmother volunteered along with a friend at the hospital, shuffling through the long corridors with heavy metal carts, distributing donated paperback books to the patients. I was intrigued to learn about this side of my grandparents.

I knew my grandfather was conservative from comments made by a radical activist friend, Hardy Desai, with whom I would become intimate. His father, Barney Desai, who had grown up Indian in South Africa but had been legally reclassified as a "Coloured person," took on a prominent leadership role in The South African Coloured People's Congress, an activist group fighting apartheid. He had been living in exile from the time of the anti-pass protests and Mandela's imprisonment. First settling in England and becoming a barrister "specializing in the defense of blacks in criminal cases," he moved to Zimbabwe in 1986, where he developed a stronger tie to the Pan Africanist Congress, for whom he would later serve as a publicity secretary and negotiator in the post-apartheid constitutional talks of the early 1990s.[12]

The first evening that we spent together, Hardy commented bluntly: "Your grandfather was quite conservative."

I knew he was right. My grandfather did not think native Africans could successfully rule themselves. While he believed in their independence and had great respect for the Shona customs, their ethics, and cultural practices, he held a patronizing view of their ability to perform in a "white man's world." I also learned that my grandfather viewed the Shona people as unduly superstitious, despite his endless investigations into their traditions and customs. Had he lived through Mugabe's dictatorship, he would have undoubtedly felt justified and equally as heartbroken. No one had anticipated that Mugabe, the tall, charismatic Oxford-educated emancipator, would become such an unerringly brutal and indomitable force, willfully starving his people, stoking tribal differences, and thereby squandering the potential of this fertile and dynamic region. Only weeks after my arrival in Zimbabwe, Nelson Mandela was freed and apartheid officially ended. Hardy and I then spent some time together in South Africa, where he would visit his father's birthplace for the first time.

---

12 "Rissik Haribhai 'Barney' Desai." Rissik Haribhai "Barney" Desai | South African History Online, *South African History Online*, 17 Feb. 2011. Web.

Family money

Having never spoken openly about my mother's illness, I refrained from asking my grandmother about its onset. I never asked whether my mother's illness might have caused her or my grandfather distress. I believed that concern for my mother, for the difficulties she faced living alone on a very limited income, never came up. Only upon rereading a hastily penned journal from my travels while writing this book was my memory jogged on this subject.

"Your father isn't giving your mother enough alimony," my grandmother complained to me one day as we sat outside in her garden. "You must press your father to pay more. She supported your father in his early years, and was there for him."

I could appreciate her rationale. His career-making invention was conceived at Bell Labs. My mother had supported him in his decision to leave England to take a research post in America. Perhaps she deserved a more generous share of his earnings after twenty-five years of marriage. The topic for me, however, was a contentious one. I did not see how I could achieve any great sea change as the mediator of my parent's divorce. My father made a living as an academic, which meant he was remunerated with consistency, but not lavishly. Now financially secure, married to someone new with whom he would start another family, he surely wouldn't welcome additional expenses. My father's professional interests circumvented the pursuit of money. His early experiments had been generously funded by the postwar investments of both corporate and government supported R&D in the sciences. Profit was not the goal. For my father, most investments outside of the lab were troublesome and suspect, although I imagine he took his stock investments seriously. In this case, perhaps he might have provided more generously for my mother.

I understood my grandmother's torment on this subject. My mother worked hard to live within her means, and I often wondered why no one in my mother's immediate family offered her any visible means of economic support. After independence, in order to protect the economy from "white flight," it may not have been legal for my grandmother to transfer money out of the country. If it had been, might my mother have been granted a greater share of her mother's invested income? I am not entirely sure.

March 1990

The closest my grandmother and I came to a considered exploration of my mother's illness was when I found a copy of *Wide Sargasso Sea*, Jean Rhys's heart-rending postcolonial novel reworking Charlotte Bronte's *Jane Eyre*. My mother had insisted at perhaps too young an age that I read Bronte's unsettling proto-feminist work. This book held a certain sway over me. Mr. Rochester's "violently insane" former wife hidden away in the attic would soon become a stand-in for my mother, who after her divorce would become a former first-wife, and at certain times, a well-guarded secret.

Ironically, here in my grandparents's library was the prequel to Bronte's classic, one that exposed colonialism's cruel legacy through the reimagined portrayal of Rochester's first wife, a Creole woman of mixed race whose white husband slowly rejects her and locks her away, causing her to become paranoid and to disintegrate mentally. The harsh realities of power and inequality between the genders are exposed along with painful themes of racial assimilation and white privilege. The fragmented stream-of-consciousness tale, told from the point of view of Antoinette Cosway as she is driven "mad," mirrored the profound agonies I had come to associate with my mother and her shifting cultural identity.

Sleeping in the very room my mother had occupied as a child, and where she had later spent time stabilizing after a difficult divorce and demanding treatment, I had many unanswered questions. How did my grandmother view my mother's illness? Did she believe that it was hereditary? Did she consider what kind of psychological impacts on my mother's condition came from factors such as the family's impossible standards, or the distant schooling in England, ten thousand miles away? Did she believe that the Gelfands were somehow cursed because of the role we had played, however "humanitarian," in colonializing Rhodesia? Did she feel that my mother, as the first woman in the family to pursue a career in a male professional world, suffered an intolerable strain?

Surely, I thought—handing this book over to my grandmother, whose rapt reading of this work took place over the course of a single night—we will now have *that* conversation. However no dialogue transpired between us beyond the novel's powerful literary appeal—no acknowledgment about the power distortions of colonialism that might endanger the psyche of the oppressed or the oppressor, much less the likelihood of my mother's illness having a genetic factor, thereby endangering me or my descendants. We only spoke about the book for its lyrical language and unforgettable story, nothing more.

Later I tried my luck another way.

In a taped interview I conducted with my grandmother one afternoon, as we sat together on her veranda shortly after a burst of afternoon rain, I asked her, "If you had your life to live all over again what might you change?"

"Nothing," she said self-assuredly.

"Nothing?" I tried another way. "What about work? Would you have chosen a different occupation?"

"No," she said and lightly petted the smooth-coated dog curled in her lap. "I would do things exactly the same. I would help Mike with his career, and I would type up his things."

No confession about her regret over my mother's undiagnosed illness, or her middle daughter's tragically botched suicide attempt, would be forthcoming. I was astounded. Wasn't she grossly aware of the inequities women faced in her era? Didn't she want to say *something* on the subject of my mother's illness? Admit to the discomfort in having done nothing to help her daughter seek treatment for a several years's long psychosis?

During these three months, as I traveled back and forth from her home in northern Zimbabwe to Johannesburg and Cape Town with my activist friend Hardy, and hitchhiked through rural portions of the two countries not yet electrified, Granny Esther worked almost daily on a memoir, one that she typed and retyped on a small travel typewriter, sending drafts to a relative in Johannesburg for review. More than a decade after my grandmother's death, I tracked down a copy of the bulk share of this unpublished work. Again, I found no mention of my mother's illness, nor as far as I could tell any other calamity that her family faced. The high points—her marriage to Mike, trips to the Lake Country in England, and her husband's professional accolades—filled the typed pages, front and back. No recording whatsoever of her daughters's many challenges.

6

relapse and recovery

I moved several times over the next twelve years—first from Los Angeles in 1992 to New York for graduate school, where I had the opportunity to spend consistent time with my mother. When living on an adjunct's part-time salary in Brooklyn became intolerable, in 1996 I went back to San Francisco, where I published a weird fantasy novella, *Black Market Babies*. Distributed by comics publisher Last Gasp, its subjects were triplet sisters separated at birth who unexpectedly reunite in college to embark on the nearly impossible task of finding their birth mother. Soon the high rents of San Francisco proved too difficult, and I found myself living in Los Angeles, where friends in the arts made finding a good bohemian apartment more likely.

By 2000, I was once again settled in Silver Lake, adjuncting wherever I could find work. Meanwhile, on the East Coast my mother was facing a difficult time after another psychiatrist had again reduced the amount of Haldol she was on, hoping that this would in turn decrease the harmful extrapyramidal side effects, most noticeably the tardive dyskinesia she suffered from. She had been taking her medication diligently for over ten years, faithfully combating those inner voices that insisted she was well enough to stop taking her pills. Each day, she would pour out the contents of her prescriptions onto her bed and count backwards from the purchase date with an eye to the calendar and the day of the drug's purchase. In this way, she avoided double dosing herself or mistakenly going without her medication.

Her relapse was a great disappointment to everyone. After she had been admitted to a nearby hospital, her psychiatrist of thirteen years apologized to my brother for his mistake then fled, embarrassed, never to return a call or to be heard from again.

Unfortunately, the infamous push for deinstitutionalization that began with the 1965 passage of Medicaid through which states were "incentivized to move patients out of state mental hospitals and into nursing homes and general hospitals because the program [would now] exclude... coverage for people in 'institutions for mental diseases,'"[13] meant that obtaining appropriate help for our mother would be a constant, demoralizing battle.

After a month-long hospital stay, despite the fact that the severity of her psychosis had not ebbed, the hospital informed my brother—who held power of attorney—that they would not provide her further treatment, despite being insured. At that time, the grim reality was that hospitals had the right to refuse treatment with a doctor's consent, positing that the mental health patient cannot readily be cured. John had no choice but to acquiesce. After she was admitted to a second hospital, it was suggested he have my mother transferred to long-term care; however, with its distressing costs and poor outcomes, this was a less than desirable option. Instead, he followed the advice of a social worker and had our mother admitted to an assisted living facility. At $4,000 a month, this was a costly solution that put our mother's limited savings in jeopardy.

Automatically, she was placed on a heavy dose of Risperdal, an experimental antipsychotic infamous now for its many negative side effects. Still suffering from persistent delusions, hardly eating, and now embarrassingly incontinent, she began to waste away.

---

13 Pan, Deanna, et al. "TIMELINE: Deinstitutionalization and Its Consequences." *Mother Jones*, 24 June 2017. Web.

It was roughly then, in late spring 2001 that I came from Los Angeles to visit her in this clean and tidy, large multistory facility. For most of the day, she lay listless in bed; interaction was almost impossible. I returned after the first evening to a nearby hotel, hopeful that over the course of my short stay she might regain some of her previous composure so that we might join the other residents in the facility's van for an excursion downtown to enjoy lunch and a movie together. This was not to be. She rarely left bed and was unable to hold a conversation of over two or three minutes long. One afternoon, she mysteriously rose from her stupor to take a seat on a stiff-looking upholstered chair in the quasi-elegant airy recreation room of the ground floor before a large television set to watch an international tennis tournament. In a near-somnambulant state, she clicked her fingers with excitement, remarking at the appropriate times on the skill level of the participants, after which she promptly returned to bed. During the tennis match, she was single focused. Her attention was on the tennis players; my presence was effectively ignored.

Disappointed, I spent the remainder of my visit in the third-story office with the head nurse hoping, through idle conversation, to affect a situation I was ill-equipped to change.

December 2001

Eventually our mother, famished and exceptionally thin, had a dramatic fall and was taken to a nearby hospital. The medical staff confirmed my brother's suspicions: my mother's troubling incontinence and dazed mental state were a direct effect of being placed on Risperdal. She was taken off the drug and placed back on Haldol. Immediately she stopped wetting herself and was no longer distant and unreachable. Not fully stabilized, she was released into my brother's care in Princeton housing, where he was staying with his fiancée.

She suffered from several delusions at this time. One that would resurface over the course of the next two relapses was a delusion that her teeth were falling out. In this specific case, they were melting. She refused to eat anything she deemed too hard, like cereal or crusts of bread. Later, my brother determined that while she was staying at the assisted living facility, unable to care for her hygiene, a milky film from the nutritional drinks she had been encouraged to imbibe had built up on the surface of her teeth. In this sense her delusion, like most of her past disturbances, was rooted in reality.

At this time, I was struggling with a crisis of my own, having quit a poorly administrated job and being wholly unprepared for the insecurity of being a part-time academic in a post-9/11, dotcom-crash economy. Broke and on edge, I flew to the East Coast, this time in December, to visit.

In this small one bedroom dwelling set within a lightly forested knoll, where I stayed with my mother, brother, and his fiancée, I fulfilled the need of my mother's paranoia for a suspicious actor. Constantly at loggerheads, my mother and I plunged back in time to those acrimonious years before she received treatment. She was agitated, hostile, and accusatory. Once again, I was her adversary. As it snowed outside, my brother's fiancé attended classes at a local community college and my brother studied for arduous exams; meanwhile, my mother paced manically back and forth inside the six-hundred-square-foot abode, accusing me of inanities (*You stole John's money, I saw you. — Where are you going dressed like that?*), before making demands on my brother for his attention regarding her latest delusions in which scandal-ridden and recently bankrupted Enron Corporation figured strongly.

Pre-existing conditions

A few weeks later, after I had returned to Los Angeles, my brother became overwhelmed by my mother's frantic and unimproved state. She was writing obsessively to Bausch & Lomb, complaining that their eye drops had caused her to go blind. After another bitter argument over her refusal to eat—an ongoing dilemma—he dialed 911 with the intention of having my mother committed, but then, suddenly changing his mind, hung up before anyone answered.

"Luckily," as my brother tells it, "the police came anyway." Deemed an imminent danger to herself, she was taken to a hospital roughly sixteen miles away for treatment and was involuntarily committed.

It was here that my brother learned from the medical staff about a new law passed in 1992 by Governor Christie Whitman making it illegal for hospitals not to treat pre-existing conditions. Researching her Blue Shield insurance policy, my brother discovered our mother had signed on after the new and historic law went into effect, therefore she could not be refused care after a short commitment period, a typical limitation of mental health insurance. The former hospital's refusal to care for our mother had been illegal. This bit of information would be crucial going forward. Once it was clear that the staff could not care for our mother, she could not just be shuttled off to an expensive assisted living center or long-term care facility. The hospital was required by law to find her appropriate care. Another psychiatric facility in the same county was then suggested as a good alternative.

January 2002

It was here, at this third hospital, that she repeatedly made her terrifying pronouncement: *I am going blind, Claire. Soon I will be blind.*

Each time I called the hospital that January, my mother's distress was that much more acute, her impending blindness of even greater certitude.

These terrifying delusions reminded me of the same paranoiac proclamations made by Nathaniel, the protagonist in E. T. A. Hoffman's renowned fantastic story of 1816, *The Sandman*, who by story's end will throw himself off a bell tower in an uncontrollable fit of outsized fear. My mother's "blindness" was a delusion much like Nathaniel's fear of a folkloric Sandman whose job it was to steal misbehaving children's eyesight in the middle of the night. The event that precipitated my mother's "blindness" had been an eye infection she contracted during what would be one of her many harrowing relapses. Despite the careful administration of the medicated eye drops by my brother's wife, the infection returned. One eye would become permanently slatted. Even so, she was in no way going blind. The damage was not to her eye, but to her eyelid. In her paranoid state, however, the injury manifested as a powerful delusion. Just as concerning were the ensuing delusions of a painful broken arm and total paralysis of her spine.

Days passed. Our medical options at this facility were exhausted. We were told she would have to be placed in an overcrowded long-term state facility ominously named Greystone Park. Built in 1876, it was originally dubbed the State Asylum for the Insane at Morristown. My mother was no happier about this than we were, but no matter the amount she was prescribed, no matter how many shots, Haldol no longer did the trick. New second-generation anti-psychotics were tried. None of these provided our mother with any relief.

My brother did some research on the institution and called to tell me.

"You would not believe how many of their patients have committed violent crimes. Greystone is not a good option for Mom."

"This is terrible," I fretted, unable to fathom the horror of visiting my mother someplace she would never be permitted to leave.

After months of false starts, we began to think that our mother might never recover and regain her independence. Then my brother took it upon himself to perform some independent research on our mother's behalf, uncovering a new antipsychotic medication—Seroquel—through a brief Internet search. My brother persuaded my mother's doctor, after much hesitation, to give the new drug a chance. Administered Seroquel, the mother we had lost sight of for a good part of a year began to resurface.

"I don't want to go to Greystone," she confided to me over the phone soon after the drug's administration. "If I end up there, I won't ever see you or John again."

"Probably not," was my blunt response.

I couldn't imagine visiting my mother in a psychiatric hospital where improvement or recovery was anomalous and highly unlikely. Perhaps selfishly, the institutional life was not something I wanted for our mother. For all of her daily constraints—the difficulty she had in placing her trust in other people, in driving back and forth on streets she had navigated for decades, in the making of the simplest decisions without sifting through endless, niggling worries—our mother had succeeded in leading a reasonably independent life. While she may not have been very organized (there was always that surfeit of blue jeans, papers, and sundry other domestic items that would eventually take over her living space), she managed fairly well on her own. For two decades, she had lived in New Jersey without the comfort or support of close friends or immediate family, on a modest budget. In a matter of days on this new drug, the powerful and persistent delusions that had dogged her existence for the good portion of a year would begin to recede.

I knew she wasn't actually going blind or becoming paralyzed. Even so, I agonized. If she believed this was so, then it might as well be true. It is well documented that people suffering from schizophrenia feel pain when in the grip of a powerful delusion, even when there is no actual physical injury. At night, I lay awake stricken, imagining my mother strapped to a gurney, trapped inside a failing body, on the cusp of going blind, fully conscious and unable to change her situation.

On a new cocktail of first- and second-generation anti-psychotics—Haldol, Seroquel and the anti-depressant Zoloft—Mom made a swift recovery. For the first time, she was no longer anhedonic. This "poverty of feeling," one of the secondary features of schizophrenia, had been utterly perplexing. Rarely had my mother shown the enthusiasm for the kind of daily pleasures most of us take for granted. She had showed little interest in games, sports, any routine outdoor activities like walking or biking, shopping, or romance.

Now that the apathy associated with her illness had just about lifted, my mother routinely called me to extol the virtues of her newly found interests.

"Have you heard of Elton John? He's fantastic!"

"No, tell me about him," I said. I did not remind her of my first music purchase at five years old and the gazillion times I listened alone to Elton John's mega-hit "Crocodile Rock" on the small blue record player in the den, singing off-key to my first and favorite record.

The popular Italian classical tenor Luciano Pavarotti was another favorite of my mother's. She collected all of his performances on videotape. After so many years of embittered silence, my mother's home was filled with the joy of music. A world once shrouded in darkness was now suddenly brightly accessible.

We *love* Joy

Perhaps the greatest benefit of this new cocktail came in the form of a new friend. For the first time since her diagnosis in 1983 my mother found close companionship in a recent immigrant from Ecuador, Anita, who worked for a number of wealthy patients as a private nurse, and had, along with her architect husband, come to live in the same Chatham Township apartment building as my mother.

In no time, the two women grew inseparable. They lunched together, shopped, and shared tips on doctors and local sales. My mother was a welcome visitor in Anita's apartment. She was included at almost all family holidays and gatherings. This was a boon, considering how infrequently we visited, or how infrequently Mom made the long journey to us. *Love* had even become a daily part of my mother's vocabulary. Growing up, these kind of warm declarations had no place in our household. This could undoubtedly be said for many postwar households. Only after college, when I brought back the easy use of this expression, did it become a part of the family vernacular. To hear my mother speak of love with anyone other than family came as a welcome surprise.

Whenever I made the occasional visit to Chatham to see my mother, I would hear these declarations often. *We love Joy*, Anita's adult children would frequently comment. They would then tease my mother over their little differences, most commonly her preference of horror movies and thrillers such as Tarantino's *Pulp Fiction*, *Natural Born Killers*, Jonathan Demme's *The Silence of the Lambs*, or any action movie starring Denzel Washington, over the more mainstream fare of rom-coms and sentimental foreign films. Strong in her convictions, Mom would rather spend days on end alone in her apartment than subject herself to a film she didn't like. She was well understood by Anita's family. In fact, so much so, it was not long before her children's very occasional visits were up for review. *Why don't you come to see your mother more often? Your mother misses you,* Anita would remark whenever my brother and I would finally show up for a brief stay.

Of course, there was simply no way to rationalize our disturbing detachment: I never had a justifiably good answer for Anita and her family, and I doubt my brother did either.

Thanksgiving weekend, 2010

Another ten years would pass before our mother's next relapse. This time, however, blindness would not be in the subject line. My mother, who was then about seventy years old, had flown in from New Jersey to be with us, a yearly tradition now that my brother and I were both living on the West Coast. This annual visit suited us. Without making the tiring mid-semester journey east, we could spend at least one holiday with our mother. To be frank, it was simply easier, less challenging, to spend the holidays with our father in Pasadena—his household was more intact, the reminders of dysfunctional family life not as readily discernible. However, this year would be no cause for celebration. From the outset it was clear that our mother was in the midst of a relapse.

At my brother's Westside apartment shortly after she arrived, it was obvious she had trouble keeping track of her pills. When I showed up that afternoon to take my mother to lunch, I found my brother and mother in the midst of an argument.

"I told you already," my brother said fitfully. "You can't keep dropping your pills around the apartment." As he uttered these words, I watched him capture a rolling pharmaceutical, shortly before he dug another out from the shag rug in her makeshift bedroom, my brother's office. Her medication seemed to be flying everywhere. Laughing, Mom tried her best to scoop up the colorful pills.

"Sorry," she intoned, crouching to the bedroom floor.

"My daughter cannot be around this," he scolded, showing concern for his six-year-old whom he cared for on alternate weeks, now that he was recently divorced. My mother did her best to get her pills back in their prescription containers, but the genie was out of the bottle, so to speak.

Earlier that day on the car ride back from the airport, she had begun to share conspiratorial thoughts with John, paranoid delusions of being persecuted by the legal team of a hip-implant company she was purportedly suing in a civil action, believing that her hip implant of several years back was faulty and had been recalled. Naturally, her belief regarding this particular implant proved to be false.

In under a few hours, we realized we could not adhere to the original plan, and rather than host our mother in our respective homes, we checked her in at a local hotel. Recently refurbished and affordably priced, the Hotel Angeleno, renowned in the 1970s for its glamorous rock n' roll occupants and sweeping panoramic views of Los Angeles, was minutes by car from my brother in Bel-Air. At $150 a night, the eye-catching, cylindrical-shaped, former Holiday Inn flanking the 405 Freeway seemed to be the perfect solution.

The following day

Neither my brother nor I felt comfortable staging a medical intervention even though it was patently clear that our mother had relapsed. We held out hope that she might suddenly stabilize, that her condition was not as bad as we thought. As I drove my mother from her hotel to the Beverly Center on that picture-perfect day, she shared with me unfortunate news. In an effort once again to lessen the extrapyramidal side effects of her medication, her psychiatrist had decreased her daily dosage of Haldol from five milligrams to two. It was a decision made without our knowledge or consent. In an unusually tender voice, one filled with gentle self-regard, she revealed to me what my brother and I had suspected but had not been able to confront.

"My psych wants me to tell you that we made a mistake with my medication," she said as I descended highly trafficked La Cienega Boulevard from the Sunset Strip with its celebrity hawking billboards. "But she says you don't need to worry because I am on the right amount now, and I'll be better soon."

As the rays of bright, unimpeded sunlight bounced off glittering glass-windowed boutiques, casting long shadows over clean and virtually empty sidewalks, I weighed the probability of my mother's improvement against the prospect of another interminable commitment. I desperately wanted to believe her psychiatrist, all the while suppressing the truth.

Paradise Cove

On Thanksgiving Day, we took our mother to have a late lunch with our father and his wife. We met at The Paradise Cove Beach Café, an idyllic haunt, where popular television shows like the 1960's surf-friendly *Gidget* had been shot. Another relentlessly sunny day, it was paradisiacal in only that respect. While we managed to make our way through the restaurant for a booth with an ocean view without incident, our mother wove the path somewhat erratically, her condition clearly worse than the day before. All during lunch, our mother looked tense, weary. Her eyes were strained. No one, however, commented. The charade of normalcy was making me very anxious. I had this childish hope that someone would intervene, declare my mother unwell, and help us get her to the hospital.

My brother and I sat with her in this kitschy sun-drenched setting, remarkably obedient, making small talk, admiring through the big plate-glass windows the glittering Pacific and white sandy beach, and the thatched umbrellas under which patrons drank and laughed, as large oval dishes amassed with more holiday food than I had ever seen were plunked down before us. It stunned me, how competent we were at not addressing the elephant in the room: my mother's compromised state. After consuming less than a quarter of the Thanksgiving Day food, the inordinate amount of turkey, potatoes, and stuffing that we were expected to eat, the bill arrived. We put down our five credit cards, paid the check, and headed back into the frantically bright sunlight to our respective cars.

Nighttime driving

With each passing day, Mom became more and more difficult, more argumentative and accusatory. A simple activity, like going to the movies, became burdensome, unsettling. At a showing of *The Social Network*, chosen for its legal drama and its potential appeal for my mother, my brother and I weathered constant complaints. It was as if someone had turned back time and we were suddenly children living with her under the same roof. Nothing we did was right. My brother's driving was up for review. Our choice of movie, not right. As the night wore on, she complained of a strong pain in her hip inhibiting her ability to walk.

"My hip is broken," she kept insisting. "I am in a lot of pain." The short walk after the movie from the theater to the parking lot was perilous, her rage intensifying with each step. Despite her obvious deterioration, we failed to get her medical treatment, instead treating her illness as if it were a feature of her person.

"What a bitch," I griped.

"I can't take it," John said under his breath. "I'm never taking her to the movies again."

On the last night of her stay, we dined at West, the top
floor restaurant of her hotel, with its panoramic views
of the Pacific Ocean and downtown Los Angeles. In the
waxing dark, the flickering lights of the gridded metropolis
suggested a prelude to my mother's imminent airborne
departure. Glamorous types occupied the neat upholstered
booths: an immaculate, sultry young woman in a mini skirt
and staggeringly high stilettos, whose physical presence
suggested whirlwind evenings of being feted in tinted-
window limousines, enjoying courtside tickets at basketball
games; rock musicians in t-shirts and low-profile jeans were
indulging in bottle after bottle of champagne.

While my mother had dressed elegantly for dinner, she
seemed to be in a particularly agitated and disconnected
state. We plodded through the meal as she struggled to eat
a reasonable portion of her roasted chicken. Time seemed
to drag. After paying the bill, we descended in the elevator
for her room on the fourth floor. Once inside, I began to
help her pack for her return home to New Jersey, when she
promptly discovered that she had lost her house keys. While
helping her search for her keys, I became privy to a host of
traps set for her by the hip replacement company and their
lawyers. These included acts of spying and the recording of
her phone conversations. She was animated, energized, in a
highly voluble state.

"They won't stop me. I know where they are hiding," she
announced. As I worked to keep up with her, darting back
and forth between the bed and bathroom in the bordello-
like lighting, I found her stories of subterfuge utterly
charming: what I deemed to be evidence of a rich inner
life. My mother rarely confided in me this way, if ever. Her

admissions felt delightfully intimate despite their foreboding implications. Regardless of the "rapport," I should not have permitted her to take that flight to New Jersey that following morning. Instead, I should have insisted that she be hospitalized in Los Angeles, where I would have been able to monitor her treatment. Once again, I let the disease win. Too afraid to confront my mother with the truth, too timid to call 911 and have her hospitalized, I left my mother that evening to prepare for her flight home in the midst of a deep, persistent psychosis: allowing her illness to play itself out an inconceivably long distance away. Wanting to believe her doctor would do her job and intervene.

911

My mother returned to New Jersey, apparently under the care of her psychiatrist, who would somehow get her back on track. I could only assume this to be the case, as I certainly avoided checking on her condition. Accustomed to distancing myself from my mother's medical needs, I disassociated myself from the problem, answering her calls on occasion, periodically fantasizing about an unlikely recovery. Shortly before Christmas, I called my mother to discover she was no longer answering her phone. My mother always answered her phone. If she happened to be out, on her daily walk or running an errand, she would always call back promptly.

Immediately I called my brother. This was how I learned that she had been committed to a nearby hospital. On my mother's behalf, as he had done several times before, he had dialed 911. Whisked away by perfect strangers in the midst of a terrifying winter storm, my mother was once again confined to a psychiatric ward, alone, thousands of miles from her family, struggling in the face of a progressive illness without the comfort of a trusted doctor or a familiar face. Without family or close friends advocating on her behalf, I was not too sure she would come through this on her own.

Cardiac unit

Stunned, I began calling the distant hospital hoping to speak to her. What I discovered was alarming. No longer a psychiatric patient, after falling and hitting her head against hospital equipment, she was now a patient of the cardiac ward. Even worse, a doctor had yet to sign off on her medications. Two days without the right medication, and my mother was considerably worse. When I spoke to her, she was no longer sure of her whereabouts; it was clear how deeply confused she was. The Northeastern seaboard was blanketed by heavy snow that weekend: no doctor appeared to be on duty, ever, or at least was not reachable by phone. Voicemail messages were ignored. Several phone calls and two days later, I found someone willing to listen and take concerns about my mother's medication seriously.

A male nurse in the cardiac unit was willing to take on the arduous task of procuring a doctor's approval for the correct dosage of my mother's medication. I felt ashamed to be so far away. I wondered if my mother's psychiatrist also felt ashamed for having botched her medical care. Is this why she had failed to call?

When I finally reached my brother and asked him why he didn't tell me where my mother was, he reacted: "Just let the system do its work."

Hospitals that begin with the letter "R"

In a few days it was determined that my mother would need to be moved to another psychiatric facility. Either the hospital did not take psychiatric patients for long, or they did not accept her insurance. Whatever the reason, my mother would be sent to Ramapo Ridge, a private psychiatric hospital. My brother and I had no idea what to expect. We had not been asked our opinion on the matter and had no recourse. This was presumably the best nearby facility with a bed.

It turned out to be a better facility than I could have hoped for. Overlooking tree-lined Sicomac Avenue, perched on several rolling acres, the small psychiatric facility was located in Wycoff, New Jersey, a wealthy suburb twenty miles outside of Manhattan. This was a Christian-run facility with both general adult and geriatric psychiatric care programs housed in one of several plain red brick buildings. A day after my mother had been deposited here, I arrived in the aftermath of an historic Mid-Atlantic Nor'easter that had blanketed the entire region in twenty inches of snow. The timing of this—the start of a new semester—couldn't have been worse, personally. Teaching part-time at two art colleges while maintaining another position at a community college, I had little time to prepare for the new Cultural Studies course on the science fictional grotesque that I had proposed the semester before. I felt, however, that if I did not show up for my mother it was unlikely that she would receive adequate care. After arriving at Newark, I took a cab straight to the psychiatric facility, where I found my mother in her room strangely slumped on one of two twin beds. She had lost a considerable amount of weight already. Her hair was no longer brown but patchy and grey. Her facial features, once commanding, exotic even, were now stern and drawn.

Though I suffer from an inordinate fear of medical facilities of most any kind, to my relief, the red brick facility was almost cheery. The walls painted in agreeable earth tones, the furnishings clean and new looking. Her room did not evince the tiny, cell-like room similar to where she was first committed when I was a young college student. However, like the psychiatric ward at UCLA, monitored doors and security locks prohibited patients from leaving at will, but at least the surrounding hallways and rooms were spacious and inviting.

My mother's main trouble at this point, beyond her psychosis, was the high blood pressure associated with the increased dosage of Seroquel.

On the bed, curled up in a tight fetal position, my mother appeared either depressed or catatonic. Immediately, I worked to get her up and into a seated position. After being bed-ridden for the past week or two, she was fairly wobbly on her feet. But in a short time, she was able to take short walks with me throughout the ward. Being in my company seemed to help. In just a few hours, she had pulled out of a withdrawn and listless state.

Dining room

One of the first effects of a prolonged relapse is the loss of appetite. Before returning to the hotel that evening, I escorted my mother to the dining room, hoping to hustle up support for her among the young uniformed staff. Having spent time with her once, however briefly, during a stint in assisted living, I knew she would eat soft, white foods. I tried to inform a few of the staff members of my mother's preferences when unwell: basically, gooey white substances like ice cream and oatmeal. Throughout the meal, I watched the staff's interest in other patients take the form of small plastic bottles of orange juice or short cartons of chocolate milk, while my mother seemed to vanish inside the large institutional room. We take for granted being able to "put on a face," how much a simple smile or clean brightly-colored sweater might afford us in our daily interactions. Withdrawal and apathy, symptoms of my mother's illness, caused her to disappear in a hospital environment.

At this one meal, I purposefully seated us at a table with two young women in their early twenties as much for my mother's sake as for my own. The young college-aged women were friendly and unabashed about being in my company. This automatically dispelled some of my discomfort, the prejudice I had unwittingly developed about those who suffered from neurological disruptions. My mother, on the other hand, was not capable of much interaction. Before going to the dining room, she had confided in me a fear of being shunned.

"They won't want me there," she said in a hushed voice. Numb to my mother's lifelong challenges, I wasn't entirely sympathetic, insisting she go anyway.

"This place is really nice," I ventured, making small talk.

"Oh yes," one of the college-aged girls wearing her hair in short braids, brightened, nibbling at a hamburger. "Compared to where we just came from, it's a four-star hotel."

"I think it's nicer than my apartment," I confided ruefully of my dilapidated, 1920s bohemian courtyard apartment that I was desperate to jettison.

The pair then launched into terrifying stories about a nearby state facility, where they had been confined before coming to Ramapo Ridge.

"It was terrible," the older of the two shuddered. "We were strapped down, and they yelled at us. There were no windows."

I had no reason to discount their story. This recently acquainted pair had just touched upon an unspoken fear of mine: that one day, my mother would end up in such a place, living out her final days in an environment of unmitigated filth and unbridled abuse.

A difficult decision

On the second day of my visit, my mother's doctor arranged for a conference call with my brother to devise a strategy for my mother's care. At 10 a.m. in a small room of the hospital, my mother, her psychiatrist, and I sat together at a large table, peering at a corporate multi-line phone on the table. Once my brother's voice sounded from the conference phone, the meeting began.

"I think we should first try electroconvulsive therapy," the doctor suggested. "We are getting very good results with ECT, and it won't negatively affect your mother's blood pressure like Seroquel." As the doctor spoke, my mother lowered her gaze to the institutional blue sock-like slippers with the nonslip adhesive strips that she had been advised to wear.

"That sounds like a good idea," I chimed in. She continued to gaze downward, and shook her head no.

I was baffled. "It's much better than it used to be," I tried to explain.

"Yes," her doctor said, speaking up for the improved use of this procedure substantially modified through the use of a brief pulse device.

"No," my mother refused. "I won't." I was crushed.

Unfortunately she had developed a prejudice against ECT. This was understandable. Notoriously overpowering in the 1940s and 1950s when it first gained popularity in psychiatry, it has been portrayed as causing severe convulsions, fracture or displacement of bones in some cases, and memory loss and confusion. Its portrayal in the media as largely torturous, unnecessary, and barbaric, most memorably with the "shock shop" of Ken Kesey's *One Flew Over the Cuckoo's Nest,* along with the advent of pharmaceutical solutions, contributed to its waning use.[14] My mother also perhaps retained a memory of its stigmatizing use when she had her first psychotic break in the late 1950s while studying for her college final exams. Today, electroconvulsive treatment (ECT) is touted as very much improved with far fewer side effects. I have heard stories of its positive use. A friend whose brother has suffered from severe bipolar disorder, often going off his meds with terrifying results—crashing his car into the side of a building, putting tens of thousands of dollars of debt on family credit cards—became stable only after undergoing ECT.

That morning at Ramapo Ridge there was not much time for debate. Her fears or prejudices against this treatment

---

14 Seiner, Stephen J. and Bragg, Terry A. "ECT: A History of Helping Patients." *The Huffington Post*, TheHuffingtonPost.com, 1 Nov. 2017. Web.

ran too deep, so we moved on.

Her doctor's next suggestion was to try Zyprexa, "the latest antipsychotic." Later I had to wonder what he meant by this, when he said it was a new drug, since the second-generation antipsychotic had been widely available since 1996.[15] Was its newness the form of its dispensation?

"This is a very easy drug to take," he advised, producing a dissolvable, translucent blue strip similar in appearance to newfangled breath mints or mini Post-its.

While my brother in Los Angeles listened in, the doctor demonstrated for my mother how to take Zyprexa.

"Joy, you just place it on your tongue and let it dissolve." Again my mother vetoed his suggestion.

I felt let down by my mother's behavior. Why was she so obdurate? I felt equally disturbed by her doctor's suggestion that my mother place an unfamiliar blue object on her tongue. Was this the right tack to take with someone suffering from paranoid delusions? A few moments passed before my brother and the doctor agreed: the first course of action would be the Zyprexa. I felt utterly confused. Hadn't my mother just said "no"?

New to the vagaries of my mother's healthcare, I kept silent. Later, when I talked with my brother privately, he explained the importance of establishing respect for the doctor's decisions.

"We don't really have a choice," he clarified. "Ultimately her healthcare is up to him, not us."

---

15 Citrome, Leslie et al. "A commentary on the efficacy of olanzapine for the treatment of schizophrenia: the past, present, and future." *Neuropsychiatric disease and treatment* vol. 15 2559-2569. 5 Sep. 2019, doi:10.2147/NDT.S209284. Web.

The patriarchy

The next morning I awoke to news heralding another major New England blizzard, one on par with the Nor'easter that had paralyzed the entire metropolitan area just the previous week. This made finding a taxi to take me from my hotel to my mother's hospital nearly impossible. From the moment the stout Russian cab driver ducked into the lobby of the Woodcliff Lake Hilton and trundled up to the front desk, half-covered in snow, I knew I was in trouble.

"I'm not going back out there," he announced gruffly to his friend behind the front desk. "Nothing will make me do it."

After a number of calls to several other car services, the front desk clerk finally found someone willing to drive me the short distance. Arriving late to the hospital that morning, I was just in time to discover that my mother had refused the new medication. Crestfallen, I did not display much patience.

"Please, I've come all this way to help you," I beseeched her to follow the doctor's orders. "Do it for me. Just try it."

My mother's pleasure in defying her doctor was undeniable. Her grin told me as much. This behavior took me back to my childhood when we lived together under the same roof in the suburbs of New Jersey, to a time when my mother would take regular pleasure in defying the simple household rules set by my father during the Carter years, when energy efficiency was a national objective. *Joy*, he would complain. *Who put the heating up*? She would lie about her wasteful energy use, *I didn't put up the heating—Claire did it*, placing the blame on her twelve-year-old daughter, when we all knew she raised the thermostat by several degrees whenever she got out of the bath and felt cold.

"He's not a good doctor," she complained to me about the Ramapo Ridge psychiatrist after refusing to take her morning Zyprexa. "He's not as smart as he thinks he is."

"Great. Don't listen to your doctor," I chided unhappily. "Stay here in this hospital for the rest of time."

Yes, I knew that paranoia was a feature of my mother's illness yet I couldn't help but question her underlying motives. What precipitated her sense of superiority? Was her rebellion racially motivated? Did she lack respect for her doctor because he was Indian and not Jewish or Anglo like her previous doctors? Or was this a subconscious jab at her long-since-deceased father? Was she thumbing her nose at her doctor as a means for asserting herself against the patriarchy? Getting back at the world for her many terrifying losses? Or was she simply protecting herself from another inefficacious treatment?

Increased dosage

At this juncture, her doctor had no choice but to administer to her a sizeable dose of Seroquel: six hundred milligrams. To counterbalance my fears of a bad reaction, I spent the day shepherding my mother on short walks throughout the small hospital. Looking for distraction, we spent time in the community rooms. In the large sitting room, where windows opened out upon a wintry scene of snow-blanketed hills and mature oaks, there was an abundance of daylight. We sat together on a large couch stationed across from a huge flat-screen television. The loud TV—which was set to unsettling fare of unsolved true-crime murder mysteries—soon got on my nerves. A second community room, smaller and adjacent to the nursing station, attracted a more sophisticated set.

The bright winter light was softer here, mitigated by white gauze curtains. On this quieter television, 1970s dramas starring Robert Redford played throughout the day.

The room that held the most horror, we were to soon discover, was windowless and located at the far end of the ward. Somnambulant, prone geriatric patients were splayed in strange positions in long metal mobile contraptions. I warned my mother to steer clear of this particular room. I feared the private institution would keep her here, ad infinitum, thereby enriching themselves and draining her of the last of her precious Medicare days. We did not have long-term care insurance and were afraid the officials might deem this necessary for our mother should she not improve.

During these short walks between wards and community rooms, I noticed my mother's diminished physicality and concerning lack of balance. Her elastic-waist sweat pants, size "small," were alarmingly baggy. Another fall was all but inevitable. This worried me, but no one I spoke with seemed too concerned. That day, I approached my mother's social worker sitting behind the front central desk in the geriatric ward.

"Can you get my mother some sort of help? She's going to fall again if a nurse or someone doesn't help her. I'm leaving for California tomorrow, and I won't be able to return for another few weeks. She has no family here in New Jersey."

Carol, my mother's social worker, assured me she would get a nurse's aide to watch over my mother. Despite her cheerful and affecting tone, I did not feel hopeful.

That afternoon, wearied by the situation, I left several hours ahead of my scheduled flight. My excuse: the imminent monster snowstorm. The same brave man of Haitian descent who had shuttled me from the hotel to Ramapo Ridge earlier that day waited for me in his shiny black Cadillac in the short circular drive of the brick building. The storm had scaled down considerably. I was lucky. There were just snow flurries now on the highways as we drove a slow, cautious journey to Newark airport. Through the fogged-up window, I took note of the bridges, old foundries, the tall and abandoned brick tenements on the outskirts of Newark, mesmerized by the relics of America's earlier industrialization, glad to be headed home.

Brothel

No sooner did I arrive in California, with its severe ongoing drought and unfathomably high temperatures, than my mother had a significant fall. I was beside myself. I had failed to prevent it. Whisked away to a nearby medical hospital, she was alone once again with no one to monitor her surroundings. According to her social worker, the high dosage of Seroquel she had been taking had caused her blood pressure to skyrocket, just as we feared. Lightheaded and dizzy, she had fallen down on the way to breakfast. After a discussion with my brother, who had already contacted the administration of Ramapo Ridge in order to get them to consider her condition more seriously, I called the hospital to speak to her.

"Mom, are you okay?" I asked once I got through.

"Yes. I think I am in a bottle." Her voice was slurred. She almost sounded drunk.

"What?" I could not follow. I tried to picture what might be happening. Had she just returned from an MRI? Was this what she meant? "You're in a bottle?" I repeated back her words.

"No," she corrected me. "I'm in a bro*thel.*"

In the background I could hear peals of girlish laughter.

Were these nurses heavily made up? This was New Jersey after all. I decided that they had to be. My mother's use of the antiquated term *brothel* made sense given her background and present state of mind. Still I was not comforted by the open mockery of the attending nurses. I felt anxious and scared for my mother. *She shouldn't be alone in the hospital. Someone should be there who can advocate on her behalf.*

I've killed John

Anxious, I began a heavy regimen of exercise. At night, I would take long walks around the Silver Lake reservoir, climbing steep cement staircases that cut through the hill-sides. During the day, I took Pilates classes, and it wasn't long before I overdid it and injured a knee. Cortisone shots did little to ease the swelling or the pain. Foolishly, I continued to exercise, until eventually I found it difficult to walk even the shortest distance. I had no doubt torn a ligament, but refused my doctor's request to get an x-ray after the possibility of surgery was mentioned. I was determined to keep working until somehow I mended on my own. An adjunct, I had limited access to sick days. I couldn't fathom how I would continue to make a living if I was laid up.

Meanwhile, my phone conversations with my mother grew more disconcerting. Her blood pressure had stabilized, enabling her to return to Ramapo Ridge, where she had been assigned around-the-clock nurse's aides. Now when I spoke to her, she felt compelled to confide in me that she had killed someone. This *someone* turned out to be my brother.

"I feel terrible," she would say. "I've killed John."

"No, Mom," I promised her. "You haven't killed John. You haven't hurt anyone." I couldn't help but wonder if this was the expression of a guilty conscience.

"Is this why he never calls?" she asked me finally.

A tremendous thing

Before I returned to Ramapo Ridge, my mother's neighbor and estranged friend called to tell me of her attempts to visit my mother. Apparently, Anita had been turned away from the facility twice. It was a fair distance from Chatham in Morris County to Ramapo Ridge in Wycoff, over an hour by car. I was saddened to hear that my mother would not permit her friend to visit. Anita had brought to the hospital clothes that my mother needed from her apartment. Underwear. Nightgowns. I hadn't accomplished much shopping on my mother's behalf. My shipment of clothing was late, and not entirely complete. My mother was lucky to have such a caring friend, and I wished she could find it in her heart to see her, though a number of minor disagreements in previous months had precipitated an unfortunate strain on their relationship already.

Sharing my disappointment with my brother, he reminded me that my mother's reaction was perfectly understandable.

"In this condition, she won't want anyone to see her like this. She feels ashamed. They will be friends again. Once she's feeling better. You'll see."

My mother's consistent refusal to answer her friend's phone calls over the next week told me otherwise. The advantages of staying in New Jersey with its familiar set of circumstances—doctor, local stores, and a best friend and daily confidante—were slowly coming to an end for my mother. This seemed more than evident.

A final visit

After fielding phone calls from concerned family members, I packed for another short visit to New Jersey, afraid of what I might find. The next to call that day before I left was my aunt Anne from Texas. I was fairly pessimistic about my mother's state. After being hospitalized for more than two months, my mother had stopped taking my calls, having slipped into a near-catatonic state. My mother always took my phone calls. I conveyed my anxiety to my aunt. I confided that I didn't believe my mother would recover.

"This is it," I pronounced grimly. "She won't get better. She's lost to us."

My aunt had very reassuring words for me.

"She's gotten better before, she will get better again. You don't think she will, but she can."

Despite her confidence, I still felt dubious. Before my mother's sister hung up the phone, she asked if she could call the hospital to speak to my mother.

"Let me ask her first," I suggested, all too aware of my mother's typical prohibitions.

Prepping that night for a creative writing class I was giving
at SCI-Arc on the science-fictional grotesque, rereading Brian
Evenson's weird short story *Watson's Boy*, I experienced
a powerful sense of dread. This take on the discomfiting
1920 conditioning experiment of behavioral psychologist
John B. Watson strangely mirrored the unrelenting misery I
associated with my mother's relapse.

A victim of a disorienting physical and mental bondage,
Brey, the son of alarmingly dysfunctional parents, is
burdened by the meaningless gathering of heavy metal
keys from the intersections of endless and identical looking
hallways. Not one of these keys fits a single door. Like neural
circuitry that has been shorted, useful pathways collapse
and disappear. Brey is oblivious to the impossibility of his
task, obligingly working to gather these keys according to
his poet father's instructions. The heaviness and futility of
his Sisyphean task is exacerbated through the attachment
of these keys to a harness Brey's father has strapped to his
chest.

"He is capable of adjusting to the cruelty, to prolonging
the madness for however long, no matter the effect.... The
increasing weight of keys stunts his movement, cripples his
growth," Evenson narrates on Brey's infernal state. "He does
not resent this—he does not realize it."

As the otherwise Sherlock Holmes-inflected title suggests,
this is a detective story; but the burden Brey carries is
an impossible koan. Our protagonist is prohibited from
gathering clues, from unlocking doors. The keys do not fit the
locks. The mind cannot be illuminated. There is no escape.
In a paralyzed state on the bed, wrapped in bandages, Brey's
mother is "mummified" in advance of potential dangers, the

inevitable charge of rats: the one other vestige of life in the dank dungeon of the "family mind."

Reminiscence on a tragedy

Before leaving for the frigid East Coast the next morning, I succeeded for the first time all week in reaching my mother by phone. She now had the energy to confide in me a number of delusions. She was no longer able to walk. Again there was talk about the faulty hip replacement and her need to sue the manufacturer. She demanded I do some sleuthing online to look for a class-action suit.

I quickly changed the subject. "Anne called. She wants to know if she can call you."

My mother grew silent for a moment, then cautioned me in a hushed voice against letting her sister know where she was.

"She wants my leg," she said to my dismay. "She mustn't know where I am."

I promised not to disclose her whereabouts.

I was rattled by my mother's reference to her sister's missing leg. My mother had never spoken openly to me about her sister's tragedy. Why had she been taken over suddenly by the past? Was this survivor's guilt? Overpowering feelings she might have experienced more than forty years before? For the first time, I considered my mother's reaction as a young woman to the news of her younger sister's crushing loss. The utter confusion she must have felt upon learning that her eighteen-year-old sibling had suffered an amputation. We rarely spoke of familial pathos and certainly not without marked discord. For instance, in a frank conversation with my mother shortly after I learned of her psychiatric diagnosis, she grew defensive.

"I don't have schizophrenia," she said in an injured tone. "I don't."

She then called my brother and sought his confirmation that I had lied about her diagnosis. He soothed her somehow. I don't recall exactly what was said, only that my brother warned me, after speaking to my mother, to be more careful.

At twenty-four years old, I was no doubt tactless. Eventually she would embrace the full scope of her illness. I never raised the subject with her again.

Before the court

Over the course of the weekend I spent with my mother, she was mostly unresponsive. She spoke in monosyllables. *Yes. No.* Shocked to see her in this condition, it confirmed fears I held about the unlikelihood of her recovery. I spent the majority of the day in the large common room alone watching television with an animated woman in her sixties. Quick-witted and easy to talk to, the stout-looking woman with a blonde up-do seemed perfectly stable, as far as I could tell. We shared a number of cracks about the true crime murder mysteries blaring loudly from the cathode-ray-tube TV. What could be more ironic given that this was meant to be a therapeutic environment?

After not too long, the air of normalcy was disrupted. This lively woman confided in me that she was being held against her will at Ramapo Ridge. In explicit detail, she told me how at the end of each week she had to appear in "court" and how, each time, "the judge" ruled that she could not be discharged, even though she was perfectly fine. She must be delusional, I told myself. This form of illness was new to me. My mother's persecution complex made it impossible for her to openly discuss her fears with anyone unknown to her. This woman didn't exhibit signs of mania or depression. She did not appear "medicated."

I began to panic. What if there was some truth in what she had to say? Her fears confirmed for me complaints I had read on Yelp prior to visiting my mother here. A "patient" on Yelp had described being held hostage by this "court," a weekly tribunal held in the basement of the facility. I began to worry that my mother might never be released. Would they keep her here until she went bankrupt? I contemplated my mother's reaction when she finally learned that in order to leave she would have to go to "court" and appear before a "judge." Would this trigger in my mother painful memories of a waylaid law career? Would she then suffer another setback?

I left to find my mother's social worker.

"She won't spend the last of her days languishing here?" I asked.

"Everyone eventually leaves," she told me.

Markedly worse

The following day I returned to find my mother again in bed. On my last visit, she lit through the hallways looking for her doctor, eager in her own way to participate in her treatment. In a highly indecisive and agitated state known as aboulia, she vacillated between being in agreement and disagreement with his changes to her medication, the primary change being an increase in her anti-depressant, Zoloft. The moment she had succeeded in locating him and moved to reverse her previous position, she would invariably change her mind, and once again go looking for him. While her manic indecision was painful to witness, her present condition was markedly worse. No longer able to care for her appearance, her hair was fully gray, wild. Her pallor, chalk-white. She had lost even more weight. Whatever ability she had to care for herself when she first arrived had almost entirely vanished.

It took several hours of being woken by staff before she was able to rise. When she did, a painful scene would ensue. She would accuse her nurse aids of all sorts of abuse, refusing their help in getting dressed or to being washed. Convinced she was being beaten, it took two nurses to get her into the shower and dressed. One day, I found her nearly being dragged through the hallway coming back from the shower, her hair newly washed and combed, in loose khaki pants, shouting damning accusations.

"Ow, ow," she cried irritably, impugning her nurses. "She hurt me. She hit me, she hit me."

I began to fear that this would become a self-fulfilling prophecy.

After she had managed to eat a spoonful or two of her gloppy-looking cereal, my mother allowed me to take her on a short journey about the carpeted hallways in a wheelchair. Not in good shape after her fall, she was no longer permitted to walk through the ward without nurse aids, or a wheelchair.

"Let's sit someplace new," I blathered, intent on a change of scene.

We entered the small lounge, and I took a seat on the couch. My mother remained in her chair beside me. On the television, a sentimental 1970s drama played. Our time here would be short. Soon my mother began to complain.

"It's too smoky in here." I had guessed she would feel this way from the moment I entered the room. What appeared to me to be sunshine refracted through sheer curtains appeared not as mitigated light to my mother but smoke. A visual hallucination: its origin, an affected occipital lobe.

I tried explaining the phenomenon. I had never liked being held under the sway of my mother's fears, real or imagined.

"No, Mom. It's sunlight being filtered through the curtains."

I tried to persuade her to stay, but after some discord, finally agreed to move on. My distress must have been obvious because I was suddenly the beneficiary of a sympathetic ear. Another patient, a low-key looking man in a blue Lacoste tennis shirt, rose from where he was seated to approach me.

"Don't worry. She'll get better soon. You'll see."

I shook my head doubtfully. "I don't think so."

Another woman dressed in a long caftan echoed his well wishes.

"Oh yes, she will be better soon. Not to worry, dear."

Touched by these people battling troubles of their own, I felt a sudden ray of hope and thanked this small coterie for their kindness.

Back in the large common room, the television loud and blaring, I broached the topic with my mother about coming to live with us in California after leaving Ramapo Ridge.

Suddenly my mother began to convulse, shaking in her wheelchair from head to toe. I had never seen anyone shake like this before, least of all my mother. I felt terrible that our conversation had induced in her such a reaction and escorted her back to bed.

That night at my hotel

At 6 p.m., I perched myself at the compact two-person bar for a boozy evening. This seemed reasonable recompense for a stint at Ramapo Ridge. Located two short blocks from the Garden State Plaza and the Woodbury Commons Outlets, and twenty minutes by car from nearby Manhattan, the stucco corporate hotel was the main highlight in Woodcliff, a magnet for international travelers hoping to strike a good bargain. Seated at the black laminate bar in the foyer, I made the most of the half-warmed meal that had arrived in an unopened plastic container. There was nothing on the menu that did not come in this quick and convenient form.

After drinking more wine than I care to admit, and having finished my partially warmed hamburger, I returned to my room slightly inebriated but not nearly drunk enough to ignore my surroundings. The featureless room depressed me. At least I had learned enough from my previous visit to ask for a room that did not face the highway. This meant being spared a sleepless night of being awoken by the intermittent sound of passing trucks. I tried looking on the bright side. Unsure what I would do now in this softly painted corporate tomb, I lumbered onto the bed, snatching the remote from the night table. No sooner had I propped myself on the hard bed on a stack of foamy pillows then I received a call from a friend from my high school days in New Jersey. She had called to make sure I was not feeling too alone. I could always depend on Alida, whose gleaming acumen and steadfast tender heart saw me through most anything. We chatted for a good hour or so before hanging up. My anxiety had lessened enough after this call and an aimless scroll through lists of endless programming on television to course into a mildly antiseptic sleep.

Mom's prognosis

Shortly before my departure for California, I stopped to talk to my mother's doctor. Easy access to doctors and nurses was another commendable attribute of this facility. In the central annex, the medical staff would take turns sitting at a long desk, answering phones, administering meds, working on charts, always available to field questions, to discuss concerns with patients and family members. We engaged in a short discussion on my mother's prognosis. I was hoping to broach with him the subject of moving my mother to Los Angeles. Given her present condition, I anticipated a negative reaction on his part. She is not nearly well enough to leave, I expected him to say. Instead, he surprised me by remarking on the healing power of family.

"The psychoanalytical literature emphasizes the importance

of living in close proximity to family members. They don't know why exactly," he explained, "but it just seems to work." I seemed to be laboring under negative suspicions of my own. The staff clearly wanted to see my mother reintegrate and leave.

Despite her doctor's approval of our plan, I still wondered how she would ever convince the "judge" that she was well enough to leave. She was still suffering from a number of delusions, and there were still several requirements she had to fulfill in order to be discharged. She needed to eat complete meals. She had to become more mobile. After returning home, I still had trouble getting her to take my calls. When she did come to the phone, she confessed to me a range of disturbing delusions.

"I have been committing incest with your brother," she divulged to me more than once. On another occasion she told me her roommate had been "skinned." I found this revelation especially harrowing. Why did her delusions have to be so horrific? It didn't seem fair or comprehensible that anyone should have to endure such unrelenting phantasma- gorical terror. Why didn't her brain offer up more agreeable hallucinations? Soon she began to complain of being required to sit in "that awful room": the one with the drugged, immobile patients.

"Start eating more so you can leave," I begged.

The reports from her social worker on her progress were never good.

"Your mother is not eating her cereal, and she spends most of the day slumped over in her wheelchair."

"You have to sit upright in your wheelchair," I demanded of my mother when we spoke. "Otherwise, they won't let you leave."

To my welcome surprise, when my mother finally made the dreaded "court appearance," she did not crumble. On the contrary, her social worker reported back that once Mom knew she had to be in court, she took the whole event very seriously, dressing smartly for the occasion. The "judge" deemed her fit to leave, and we were set. The only other requirement of her release was that we find her a skilled nursing facility in Los Angeles where she would be assisted in making the transition. As it turned out, no one we called seemed to have room. Not even one nursing facility on the Westside of Los Angeles had a vacancy. We were stuck. As a last resort, I called my mother's cousin, who worked as a doctor at Cedars-Sinai, and sought his guidance. He was able to get us in touch with someone at their Rehabilitation Center, where he often worked with recovering patients. Apparently this facility had vacancies, or would consider us—I couldn't help but wonder if my mother's illness was what precluded her easy admission to a general facility.

Upon her release from Ramapo Ridge, my mother seemed no better than when I last saw her. Somehow, despite her atrophied condition, my brother managed to get her onboard an airplane. Having left the frigid East behind, at the Rehabilitation Center, she performed well, eating meals, committing to a hefty regime of physical therapy. Even so, she was still plagued by a number of persistent, disturbing delusions.

"Don't forget, Claire," she called to tell me the day before her scheduled release. "There's still the sexual problem." I would eventually learn she had come to believe she was in possession of genitalia from both sexes.

My brother was instrumental in relieving her anxiety.

"Don't worry," he told her. "No matter what, we will love you anyway." This seemed to ease her mind, and the conversation on this uncomfortable topic thankfully ceased. Once she completed her two-week stint at the Rehabilitation Center, we set about looking for health aides to help her establish a routine in her new apartment in Los Angeles.

After five months of medical attention, our mother was ready to begin a new life.

7

day-long obsession

and torment

Summer 2011

Finally, my mother would be living in proximity to her grown children. John had found a spacious one-bedroom in one of Park La Brea's seventeen Landmark Towers, the revolutionarily "X"-structured 1946 steel and concrete buildings that afforded views of the surrounding mountains and city to all of its tenants. My mother's seventh-floor apartment boasted a stunning panorama of the Hollywood Hills, from the Pacific Design Center all the way east to the Griffith Park Observatory. This glamorous complex off of Third Street, with its teeming array of urban amenities, most prominently The Grove shopping and cinema complex, seemed the perfect housing solution. In Mid-City, Park La Brea had the added benefit of being roughly thirty-minutes driving time from either my place in Silver Lake or my brother's home on the Westside.

The time of my mother's arrival luckily coincided with my summer break. I was able to visit twice a week in order to get her settled. In no time, with the help of health aides—Filipina sisters Jaime and Vanessa—our mother became acclimated to her new surroundings. She took fitness classes at the Park La Brea Senior Center twice a week. No longer driving, she was still able to shop nearby at the Whole Foods at Fairfax and Third Street, pick up her prescriptions at the CVS and spend afternoons at the historic Farmers Market and Grove outdoor shopping center.

She had even begun to take computer classes two to three times a week. We would often spend Sundays together, first at the Farmers Market, where we could get dinner at Loteria, the Mexican restaurant, splitting a delicious Summer Salad with lots of jicama and avocado, before watching a movie at the cozy Park La Brea Theater.

While she no longer benefited from living across the hall from a best friend, over the course of the following year she would spend more time with her granddaughter upon whom she lavished small treats whenever she had the opportunity. Within a year, she appeared relatively well adjusted to living in California. For the first time since graduate school, I could visit my mother with some ease.

December 2012

However, the peaceful times were not to last. It was now the holidays. After a long absence during a busy fall semester, I finally had time to spend with Mom. She had been particularly understanding of my hectic schedule for these past couple of months. Whenever I had trouble visiting due to my nonstop teaching and the occasional writing assignment, she would tell me not to worry. *That's okay, darling*, she would say. *Finish your work.* For eight weeks, she gave me a pass on our weekly visits. Living on her own, without close friends, my mother worked hard to stay occupied, filling her days as best she could.

Relations were visiting from out of town: her sister Anne from Texas had arrived along with her daughter, my cousin Lorraine. We were meant to get together that week at my mother's apartment for tea after a short visit to LACMA, the county art museum with its sprawling hodgepodge of buildings and galleries just a few blocks from my mother's apartment. Instead she had begged off, suddenly, complaining of a sudden bout of diarrhea. I had trouble believing that my mother was sick. My mother's antipathy toward her family ran deep. I half wondered if she might be purposefully isolating herself. This was further confirmed when she began to impugn another family member, her cousin who had supported her during the worst of times, her relocation from Ramapo Ridge, and those difficult first post-divorce years when she tried to live close to her children.

"Stephan gave me diarrhea. He brought the infection with him from the hospital." Stephan, who had joined us a few nights before for a family dinner in Century City after his rounds at Cedars-Sinai, was to blame for her present condition. "It's his fault. He brought bacteria from the hospital with him," she said, continuing her harangue.

It had been two days since our family get-together at her apartment had been called off. When I called to see how she was, I was surprised to learn that she still wasn't feeling much better.

"Everything is a mess," she confided in a heavy voice. "I have so much to do. I need to clean things. There's so much laundry."

I couldn't conceive of what she was talking about. Why was there so much laundry? My mother owned two sets of sheets and two sets of towels. I felt confused by her circumstances yet didn't offer her much help.

"Maybe I can visit," I suggested. "We could get dinner or see a movie."

"Not today," was her response. I grew agitated. Why didn't my mother want to socialize, even for a short period of time? She always welcomed my visits.

"Maybe when you're feeling better we can do something," I sniped.

She then complained about picking up her medication from CVS. "I had a terrible time getting my pills today," she said in a strained voice.

Again, I failed to empathize with my mother, assuming this was the prelude to a lengthy conversation about a small annoyance, a difficult person working at a cash register or a neighbor who had stopped her on the way to the store or took up too much of my mother's time bantering on an ill-considered topic, so I ignored it.

"Okay," I said. "Call me if you want to do something," and hung up disappointed.

December 22 and 23

The weekend came, and I began to worry. Why didn't she want to see me? Usually I heard from my mother at least twice a week. This week I hadn't heard from her once. I called to find out how she was. There was the mess still. And then she launched into something new.

"You mustn't drive anywhere with your friend Monica." How did we get on this topic? I wondered.

"What are you talking about?"

"That night at John's," she carped. "She was drunk. I saw her."

"Why are we talking about this?" It had been a month since we had driven my mother to an early Thanksgiving party at my brother's house. Monica was the designated driver that evening. I had had a few glasses of wine, while Monica had just one. She offered to drive my Prius home in the light rain. Unfortunately, the car skidded somewhat dangerously when she braked as a car ahead of her on windy Sunset Boulevard came to stop. Monica veered across the double yellow line to avoid a collision. Luckily, it was late at night, and there wasn't any oncoming traffic on that particular patch of road. At the time, my mother took the whole ordeal in stride. Apparently it was now a cause for concern.

"Monica doesn't drink," I hastily countered. "She has an eating disorder. She can't eat or drink, except in very small amounts."

It was true. My friend, an astonishingly talented street photographer, who had lived with this disorder for decades, rarely consumed anything in its entirety. I tried explaining this to my mother.

"I saw her," my mother snapped in defiance. "She was drunk."

Was this true? Had my friend suddenly become a lush right under my nose? Had she consumed glass after glass of wine covertly in the kitchen that night as my mother suggested?

My mother warbled on some more about my friend's bad qualities. "You mustn't go anywhere with her," she chided. Why did she have it out for Monica? Was she jealous of our ten-year friendship? "She was drunk," she repeated. "I saw her."

"I won't take you to parties anymore if you are planning on sitting there and watching us hawkishly," I said hotly.

"Fine," she snapped. And I hung up, rattled.

Back here, again

That night I had a powerful dream. In it, my mother flew
about her Park La Brea apartment on a broomstick, half
naked. I didn't want to see her this way. Swooping back and
forth over the white-carpeted space, she was in prime spirits,
laughing maniacally. Her partial attire and skin tone were
the same impossible color, a surreal Barbie-pink. As much
as I wanted to, I couldn't leave. Suddenly I felt the rounded
hard end of her broomstick being rammed into the middle
of my back. Helpless to stop her, I took several hard blows
before I awoke, gripped by an overwhelming despair. This
was the mother of my youth, unstoppable and out of control.

As the day came into focus, I sensed my mother was in
danger of another relapse. I was devastated. She had only
just recovered from her last relapse of a year and a half
before.

"Mom is acting strangely," I called to tell my brother. He
confirmed my suspicions.

"She's been calling me with strange worries too."

I then confided in him my strange dream, expecting him
to brush it off. Instead, he enumerated the countless dreams
he had had over the years, finding himself alone with our
mother in the New Jersey house where we grew up. Early
on, shortly after our parents's divorce my brother developed
the ability to lucid dream. By acknowledging the fact that
he was dreaming, he could control the outcome of these
nightmares, making contact with the symbolic parts of his
psyche. In these dreams, he would find my mother in her
bedroom, a dark curtained-off space defiled by haphazard
stacks of legal papers, strewn clothing, dirtied plates,
and glasses. *Mom*? he would ask. *Why am I back here*?
Invariably, the mother in his dream would provide him an

answer to his question: arming him with the self-knowledge that freed him from whatever constrictions he might face in his waking life.

I suggested that something might have happened to her pills. John agreed to go over and check on her. I was grateful to him for taking the drive from Bel-Air to Park La Brea, a pleasant one, but only when traffic cooperated.

An hour or so after our phone call, my brother called from her apartment.

"She's okay," he reassured me. "The pills are all here. She's not missed a day."

I thanked him and hung up, glad to hear she was okay though I was still a bit uneasy.

Christmas cake

The day after Christmas, my mother was finally up for a visit. I arrived during the afternoon in time for some Christmas cake. It turned out she had opened a holiday pastry I had purchased the week before so she would have a gift for her health aides, the Filipina sisters who had assisted her through the transition to daily life at Park La Brea, helping her to buy her groceries and navigate her new environment. I was a little disappointed to see that they had yet to receive a holiday gift, but I tried not to dwell on this.

That afternoon my mother was dressed sweetly in a white peasant top. I was happy to see her in the light clothing, taking advantage of living in California with its enviable climate. In Chatham, New Jersey she would have been weighed down in heavy sweaters this time of year.

"Sit down," Mom insisted as she slipped into the kitchen to get some plates and the cake.

Ordinarily, she struggled with her hand-eye coordination, a side effect of her medication. However this afternoon, I noted, she handled the knife especially well, cutting for us each a slice of the Belgian white-powdered Christmas cake. After a week of manic accusations, my mother was now surprisingly mellow, almost distant in her affect. Subdued, she had a slightly distracted look in her eyes. She did not speak much but was clearly enjoying the sugary dessert. I was relieved that she was in a calm mood. Seated at the white plastic-molded tulip table, taking in a panoramic view of the rippling Hollywood Hills looming in the distance, we ate in silence. I tried getting my mother to go see a movie with me, but again she declined.

"I still feel weak," was her answer.

I left shortly afterward, still concerned but nonetheless grateful for the quiet time spent together.

New Year's Day, 2013

For the remainder of the holiday season, I dated online while housesitting for a friend in Silver Lake, taking care of four semi-feral cats. Spending a good chunk of time on her couch, I watched a dizzying number of episodes of *Homeland*, discomfited by the amount of television I was capable of watching. I marveled at Claire Danes's convincing portrayal of a highly functioning spy struggling with bipolar disorder, at the same time that my mother continued to avoid family activities.

Calling on New Year's Day, I noticed a pronounced lethargy in her voice.

"Are you okay?" I asked.

"No. I can't sleep," she admitted in a hushed tone. "There are people keeping me awake."

What I had suspected for weeks was finally being voiced.

"I'll be right there." I promptly left Silver Lake for her apartment, taking the familiar route along the rutted back streets of Hoover and Temple, before turning onto Third Street, traversing the short fifteen minutes through Hancock Park with its empty sidewalks, and large single family homes in a hodge-podge of architectural styles, before reaching her place.

The first thing I did was check her seven-day pillbox. It was Wednesday, and she had not yet taken her a.m. pills. I could see that certain medication from the days before had also not been taken. This was when I realized that I did not know the exact amounts of her medication. I called my brother to find out what her required dosages were.

I learned she was required to take two hundred milligrams of Seroquel in the morning, and an additional two hundred milligrams at night. Four hundred milligrams of this powerful antipsychotic is a strong daily dosage. But after my mother's last relapse, increasing the dose significantly was the only option left to us for her stabilization. Poking through the remaining pills, I made the unwelcome discovery that instead of two daily doses of two hundred milligrams, she had been taking only fifty milligrams at a time. This explained both her insistence that she was taking her pills and the confusion we felt about her escalating aggressive and paranoid behavior.

How did this come about? I rifled through her cabinets where I found the remaining prescription and my heart dropped. The label read Seroquel fifty milligrams. The Seroquel she usually took were oblong shaped and white. These were round and peach colored. Why did the pharmacist give her these? I checked the label for directions. Nothing stipulated that she should be taking eight pills per day. The package was dated December 22. Roughly when I noted my mother's unusual behavior. "How long have you been taking these?" I asked.

"I don't know," my mother said, pacing about the narrow galley kitchen in a confused, laconic state, unable to give me a clear answer.

The best I could do was to help her immediately get a new prescription with the proper dosage.

CVS Pharmacy

After my mother's doctor called in a new prescription, I took the remainder of the prescription of fifty-milligram antipsychotic pills back to CVS. I told the pharmacist what had happened. I explained to him that my mother had been taking the wrong dosage for two weeks, and that her behavior was now very erratic. I didn't state explicitly that she was having a psychotic episode. Only that her wellbeing had been severely compromised. The pharmacist went through his computerized files, and after reviewing the label on the bottle I presented him with, he agreed that something was wrong with the prescription.

"Perhaps we were out of the two-hundred-milligram Seroquel that day, and the attending pharmacist gave her this dosage until we could get more."

I agreed that this was probably the case, but also pointed out that a second mistake had been made with the directions on the prescription.

"If this was the case, she should have been advised to take eight of these pills daily."

He concurred and promised to look into the problem in order to ensure that this did not happen again. I contemplated suing this giant corporate entity for financial recourse. Knowing what I knew about my mother's condition, I anticipated grave trouble ahead, months upon months of expensive healthcare. The out-of-pocket costs would run into the thousands. But I knew I didn't have the economic resources to take such a measure.

Instead I cut a deal. The pharmacist would give me a discount on the new prescriptions for my mother if I handed over the incriminating evidence of this tragic mistake in the form of the poorly labeled prescription bottle and the remaining pills. It was a pathetic attempt to extract some form of compensation, a $100 discount on my mother's new prescriptions, which included Haldol, the Cogentin she took to keep her from shaking, and post-hysterectomy hormones. In the scheme of things, no real compensation at all.

Chaos of night

My mother was no longer elusive. She was no longer the harpy flying about her white-carpeted apartment on a broom. Instead she was docile, willing to share with me the nature of her present delusions or hallucinations. Listening to my mother as she explained and enacted the terror she experienced alone in her apartment, I became privy to the intimate workings of a nightmare. The dividing line between waking and sleeping had been plundered, the chaos of night in full bloom.

In the short, narrow hallway between her bedroom and walk-in closet, she demonstrated for me the endless running, directly overhead, that "they" performed throughout the night. She ran in place, pumping her arms. It was a quick-paced, cartoon-like motion. I had not seen my mother animated like this before. I was relieved that she felt safe enough to share the dissolving parameters of her consciousness with me. I was also astonished. In the past her psychosis had manifested itself in the form of unfounded accusations, conspiratorial theories, life-threatening delusions. She was being pursued by corporate entities. Her teeth were melting and on the verge of falling out. Today she seemed vulnerable, almost precious. Like a young child, she was energized. Confused. She plopped down on the couch and confessed to me a host of worries, mainly about "them." Overhead pounding and loud voices were keeping her awake. She wanted to sleep but couldn't.

"Not to worry, Mom," I tried reassuring her. "You have the right medication now. In a few days you will be feeling much better."

Medicare days

John and I conferred on what to do next. I confessed that I was not up for seeing our mother go through another hospitalization and recommended that we keep her at home and take care of her ourselves. I was not adept at handling hospitals and doctors. I did not want to endure what we had gone through two years earlier at Ramapo Ridge. I did not want to encounter my mother in what is known as the "residual phase" of the illness, the one that follows the "active phase" of energetic hallucinations and delusions. I had found it nearly unbearable to watch her become what I refer to as catatonic, a state in which she was listless, inactive, and often unreachable.

"I have the time. I am only teaching two days a week this month. Why should we risk another hospitalization so soon?" I said to my brother. He agreed. We could do this ourselves.

Over a recipient's lifetime, Medicare grants those suffering from mental illness no more than six months of hospitalization. After her last relapse, my mother had only one hundred days of Medicare left. It seemed ironic. We had waited fifteen years for our mother to qualify for Medicare so that she could move to California, where medical insurance for those with pre-existing conditions had become prohibitively expensive. But now it seemed she still did not have enough medical insurance to cover her needs, even with the private supplemental insurance that she had purchased. My brother repeated this reality often, reminding me that once she reached the last of those days, she would be forced into bankruptcy. This terrified me. As a part-time instructor at a number of educational institutions, I was just able to cover my own living costs. I was not sure what I would do if my mother were to lose her access to Medicare and become a dependent of the state of California, a state that shortly after the subprime debacle appeared to be teetering on insolvency.

I considered my mother's age. She was seventy-three years old. Already she had broken one hip. Myriad medical complications could arise. What if she were to get colon cancer like her mother did in her early seventies? She had already had one hip replacement. What if she needed another? Her routine visits to the doctor did nothing to ease my mind. One doctor had recently prescribed for her a cholesterol medication renowned for its deleterious side effects. Was he not aware of the numerous medications she was already taking? My mother followed her health-conscious AARP diet to the letter. I could not understand how she could be a candidate for high cholesterol.

Then there was the fall she had shortly after moving out to California. While she might have more days to spare for physical calamities, the same was not true for psychiatric care. Another psychiatric hospitalization could cost my mother her remaining Medicare days. I was not prepared to forgo this safety net.

Secondary features

John and I devised a plan. It was essential that someone oversaw our mother's medication. On those days when I was not working, I would drive to our mother's apartment to administer her pills once in the morning, and then again in the evening until we could procure the help of new full-time health aides. My brother would help on those days he didn't have his daughter or was not commuting long distances for work. It was critical that our mother received her pills at the appropriate times and with food. A single missed pill would cause an immediate setback.

In her compromised state, everything became more difficult. Simple decisions were almost impossible to make. Activities of the most basic kind took an unpleasant amount of time. Dressing was especially hard. Mom found fault with all of her clothing. Everything smelled. It didn't matter if I had just had the item professionally cleaned. She was also convinced she smelled, no matter how often she bathed or changed her clothes.

Because my mother suffered from phantosmia, or olfactory hallucinations, she required almost daily acquisitions of new bottles of deodorant and dozens of new toothbrushes, which was particularly strange given the fact that for the past twenty-five years, my mother was loath to waste money on superfluous purchases of any kind. Living on a limited income, she had adhered to a strict budget, clipping coupons and shopping sales, rarely purchasing something extra for herself.

In addition to the endless supply of soaps and deodorants she insisted we buy, she required me to procure a limitless supply of lip balm. Dehydration was among the chief side effects of her medication. She could not drink enough water. Ordinarily, my mother maintained a healthy routine of drinking several glasses of water per day in order to combat the dehydration associated with her medication. However lethargic and confused, she could no longer maintain this protocol. To add to the misery, no brand of lip balm would suffice. The Kiehl's lip balm, Burt's Bees Lip Balm, ChapStick plain and cherry flavored, Carmex, Whole Foods Vanilla Lip Balm. Not one of these was right. Everything stung, or was deemed dirty, or was soon lost or disregarded.

Another couple of weeks

With each passing week, my mother grew more irritable and cantankerous. Her delusions only intensified, causing her to become hyper-vigilant about cleanliness. This was especially strange as she had never been a stickler for neatness. Sloppiness of any sort was unbearable. The health aide workers that we hired for a pitifully low wage were placed under gross scrutiny. Not allowed to share her refrigerator despite being there all day, they were told they had to eat outside of her apartment. Not one of her health aide workers was deemed clean enough to handle her food, or dishes, or silverware. Whenever I confronted her about admonishing these women, she claimed not to know what I was talking about. I began to wonder if her denial was related to her illness, or if she was just being stubborn.

Outings also proved difficult. One afternoon, I arrived unannounced and suggested we go for lunch.

"Where would you like to go? The Cheesecake Factory or the Farmers Market?" For as far back as I can remember, my mother's favorite restaurant to go to in Los Angeles had been The Cheesecake Factory. She also enjoyed eating at Loteria in the Farmers Market, but on this occasion it was impossible for her to make a decision. It was very difficult to get her out of the house. She was convinced that as soon as we left the apartment, her address book or her phone would be stolen. The others, or *they*, as she called them, would appear in our absence to steal her things. I had a terrible time getting her to leave her closely guarded bed. Only when I had recovered her address book and phone from the sheets of her unmade bed could I persuade her to leave.

On the short walk over to The Grove, she changed her mind a number of times about where to eat. Growing exasperated,

I finally told her we were going to The Cheesecake Factory. After taking a seat close to the balcony overlooking the busy plaza, she changed her mind again.

"Maybe we should have gone to the Mexican restaurant." She could no longer make a decision without enduring an inordinate amount of self-doubt. I wondered why she was like this. What had happened to make it so impossible for her to stabilize and make routine decisions? As she picked unhappily at her chicken Cesar salad, a dish she would have eaten with gusto just months ago, I tried consoling her.

"Don't worry, Mom. Your pills will start working soon. You'll start feeling better in a couple of weeks."

"You keep saying that," she said. "You said that weeks ago: *Another couple of weeks*," she parroted my words. Then she confided in me something I didn't want to acknowledge. "I don't think my pills are working."

I knew my mother was right. She was a bright woman and had communicated something important to me. I was unable to react properly. She was in need of a stronger dose of Seroquel, an amount that might cause her blood pressure to elevate dangerously and could only be administered to her in the hospital. Nothing my brother and I could safely give to her alone at home. Rather than pursue a conversation on the inevitable next step of another hospitalization, I focused on her eating.

"Go on, Mom. Have another bite."

Bananas

Over a month into our caretaking foray, my mother's condition continued to deteriorate. She was hostile when I arrived the following morning to help her with medication while we were between health aide hires. She didn't trust me to correctly pour out a carefully measured cup of Cheerios for her, but was no longer capable of doing this, or anything else, for herself. Before she had been able to do everything on her own. Now, dressing took hours. She insisted that her hip was broken and that she could no longer walk. When my mother was not expressing irritation or anguish with her perceived ailments, she was lying helpless and laconic in bed. She wasn't eating.

Former delusions from a previous relapse had resurfaced with stubborn tenacity. Once again, she believed her teeth were falling out, making most foods "too dangerous" to eat. She stopped eating the Lean Cuisine frozen dinners that had been the mainstay of the past thirty years, the bland one-hundred-fifty-calorie meals she purchased for under two dollars at Ralphs Market. I immediately placed her on a daily regimen of two Ensure drinks, the calorie-rich diet supplement, and even this was a battle. Because I did not routinely cook, I tried stocking her kitchen with sandwiches from Whole Foods instead. From the time she had moved into Park La Brea, she had dutifully eaten a half chicken-salad sandwich for lunch, always saving the other half for the following day. I had trouble getting her to do even this now.

"Please just take another bite," I would plead.

"The crusts are too hard," she would complain. "They hurt my teeth."

If I insisted, she would whimper, kicking her legs under

the table like a small child. Previously, she had adhered admirably to a strict daily regime of eating certain fruits and vegetables, careful, for example, to eat a banana each day to regulate her potassium intake. Now she hated bananas and screamed if I brought her a new bunch. *I don't want to look at them! Don't bring me any more bananas!*

Beverly Center

In no time, my mother and I were locked in an ugly battle. Whenever she rejected a choice of food or drink I made for her, the sparring would begin. It wasn't long before I was shouting at my mother: in the kitchen, when she would hover over me while I tried to prepare food for her; in the grocery store, when she derided all of my food choices.

It was ghastly how low I had sunk, bursting into loud, irate tears at the cash register in Whole Foods and in the Beverly Center after my mother accused the salesperson who had helped her choose some sneakers of overcharging her. I could not handle my mother's paranoid remarks, shouting like an unruly teen in public places.

"Fuck you!" I shrieked loudly in the Beverly Center, when I found it all too much to bear.

I felt agonizingly alone, despite being able to email or call my brother whenever I felt overburdened. It became clear to me weeks into her relapse that I had no choice but to write about my family history. I could not keep the torment of her relapses and my disappointment in the medical system to myself any longer. Whatever else I had hoped to accomplish in my professional life would have to wait.

Studying as much psychiatry and neuroscience on the subject as I had time to access easily between grading papers and appearing at my mother's apartment to help with groceries and other daily needs, I discovered the literature on the topic had exploded, with new memoirs on the subject of schizophrenia and schizoid affective disorder appearing monthly. Many people coping with a chronic mental disorder had taken to self-publishing.

After reading one work, I was taken aback once again at how little I understood of the actual timeline of the illness. Outlined within these pages were the powerful effects of each of three stages: prodromal (or beginning), acute (or active) and recovery (residual). Most striking was the commentary on recovery. The author of one work claimed that it took him at least a year to fully recover from the depression and mental flattening that precipitated a return to "normal." As the author described it, it was as if he were blanketed in a heavy fog for months *after* the months of intense psychosis had dissipated.

Here I was expecting my mother's return to "normal" to occur in two months. I was not prepared for her to suffer in a state of mute agitation for an entire year, and now recognized my impatience for what it was: a profound state of ignorance. After enduring months of fierce hallucinations, manic sleepless nights, and after ingesting copious amounts of anti-psychotic drugs with little to no exercise, what hope did my mother have of regaining her equilibrium after such a short passage of time? This thin, self-published memoir with its appropriately dark cover was eye opening, and I regret that in the midst of a difficult period personally and a short geographic move, it went missing.

On the shelves at the library I found more memoirs, notable biographies, medical histories, works on the history of psychoanalysis, science-focused medical tomes such as Richard Noll's *American Madness*, and works of feminist literary analysis and history including Elaine Showalter's disturbing and immensely readable study of hysteria and the treatment of women with mental illness, *The Female Malady*. Reviewing these works, not only did I come to realize how fluid our interpretation of mental illness has been, from hysteria and dementia praecox to our present understanding of schizophrenia and its biological roots, I also came to realize how poorly the treatments had worked until recently. Whether women who received treatment in the mid-nineteenth century suffered from schizophrenia or not, I cannot say, and perhaps no one will ever know. Showalter, however, details the horrifying use of "sexual surgery" or clitoridectomy on women who were institutionalized and being treated for mental illness.[16]

Overcrowded institutional custodial care continued through the late 1800s into the 1930s, when aggressive treatments such as the insulin-induced coma, which required that patients be repeatedly injected with large doses of the hormone in order to produce comas came into favor, along with electroshock, the production of seizures by the use of electric current. The lobotomy or prefrontal leucotomy was introduced in 1936. While there was some success in "calming patients," it fell out of favor after notable abuses in the 1950s when lithium and neuroleptics, first generation anti-psychotic drugs, became available.[17]

In 1959 when my mother first showed signs of this illness, neuroscience was still in its infancy. Electroshock treatment was the prevailing treatment for schizophrenia. If there

16 Showalter, Elaine. *The Female Malady*. London: Virago, 1987. 76–78.
17 Ibid. 195–219.

was no improvement, confinement to a state hospital was the next step. Reading up on these practices, none of which sounded the least bit desirable and were, in fact, quite harrowing[18] and, in some cases, deadly, I came to wonder whether my mother was privy to the same information. If so, was this partially the reason that she never sought treatment all those years ago?

The paranoid type

Doing further research, I was struck by the subcategories of schizophrenia, which include the paranoid type, the disorganized type, the catatonic type, undifferentiated, and residual.[19] Those suffering from paranoid schizophrenia were reported to be the highest functioning, at least in early editions of the *Diagnostic and Statistical Manual of Mental Disorders* and in sundry publications. People with paranoid schizophrenia are generally more capable of relating to other people and performing at work; their symptoms do not usually appear until later in life. Delusions are usually based on a central theme and continue along characteristic lines for some time. A major stressor is often the cause for those who live with the condition to experience an increased

18 Experimental filmmaker and artist Sara Kathryn Arledge (Smith) writes about her first commitment at Napa State Hospital in 1960, where she received eighteen electroshock treatments, a standard procedure, which resulted not so surprisingly in the breaking of her back. (Smith, Sara K. Ed. Terry Cannon. *Madness in Memory.* Follies. 1974.)
19 APA. "DSM-IV-TR." *Diagnostic Criteria for Schizophrenic Subtypes*, Prentice Hall, 2010. Web.

intensity in symptoms. Because they often feel persecuted, they can be quick to anger. A flat affect is not uncommon. Jocular or giddy behavior at inappropriate times, like laughter at a funeral, is a common symptom. People who suffer from this subtype category in particular fear revealing their symptoms to strangers. They can have difficulty maintaining ordinary daily activities such as bathing and brushing their hair and teeth. That this subcategory has been deleted from the DSM-V has left me more than a little perplexed.

In his notable book *Whispers: The Voices of Paranoia*, Dr. Ronald Siegel reports how the origins of paranoia are believed by neuroscientists to be located in the "limbic system": a group of neurons and hormone-secreting structures deep inside the center of the brain considered to be highly feeling. The primary features of paranoia, Siegel conveys, are "hyperalertness and hypersensitivity to the smallest details.... The paranoid becomes rigid and inflexible;" the person "is attuned to any possible threat."[20] This seemed more than evident in my mother's case. Her attention to detail was agonizing and a source of great distress. Whether it was the attention paid to a tiny bit of charred skin on a rotisserie chicken or the unfamiliar substance in a pot of boiling soup, the most-minute detail was often suspect, indicative of countless potential horrors.

---

20 Siegel, Ronald K. *Whispers: The Voices of Paranoia*. New York: Touchstone, 1996.

Organic disease

Despite my mother's long-standing diagnosis, it had been all too easy for me to slip back into "the metaphorical," as Susan Sontag has been oft quoted on the topic, and view my mother's illness as a psychological, self-perpetuating phenomenon: she was ill equipped to survive the stressors of "late capitalism" and the gender inequities in the work place and in those places that undergirded her domestic life; she was from an entitled family and therefore *destroyed* by her inability to "rate" as highly as the other top performers, the men who seemed to secure for themselves leadership roles, awards, and unassailable income. It always seemed possible somehow to fault my mother for her condition despite the hallucinations, the multiple relapses, the catatonia, the difficulty she had in making friends, or driving with confidence even though she remained squarely between the lines.

Researching the brain science, for a short while, I was able to put this view to rest. "Mental illness is not in the mind, but rather in the brain," biologist Dr. Ronald Chase tells us in his scientific memoir *Schizophrenia: A Brother Finds Answers in Biological Science*—a compassionate and determined work in which Chase weaves alternating chapters between the history and latest biomedical science undergirding the study of schizophrenia with the story of his brother's illness.

While initially schizophrenia was believed by Emil Kraepelin in the nineteenth century to be a disease of the brain, writes Chase, its neuropathology was so obscure that according to Paul J. Harrison of *Brain* magazine, it was soon identified to be "a 'functional' psychosis, a disorder with no structural basis."[21] It is only somewhat recently with CT scans and MRIs, Chase writes, that the neuropathologic basis of schizophrenia is once again of serious import. Additionally, he tells us past autopsies reveal a number of confirmed abnormalities in the brains of those who suffer from schizophrenia—for example, "ventricular enlargement and decreased cerebral (cortical and hippocampal) volume." There are other noted structural differences. Of the brain disorder from which his brother suffered, Chase writes, "The brains of people with schizophrenia show a significantly greater reduction of gray matter (the area that includes regions such as muscle control, sensory perception, memory, emotions, speech, decision making, and more) than do the brains of healthy individuals. Moreover, much of the white matter (tissue through which the communication between the different areas of gray matter in the nervous system happens) has an abnormal physical appearance in brains of people who have schizophrenia." Chase believes strongly that schizophrenia should be classified as a brain disorder and not a behavioral disorder. Like Parkinson's disease or Alzheimer's, schizophrenia should be treated as a medical illness.[22]

21 Harrison, Paul J. "Neuropathology of Schizophrenia: A Critical Review of the Data and Their Interpretation | Brain | Oxford Academic." *OUP Academic*, Oxford University Press, 1 Apr. 1999. Web.

22 Chase, Ronald. *Schizophrenia: A Brother Finds Answers in Biological Science*. Baltimore, MD: Johns Hopkins University Press, 2013.

Parsing recent neuroscience findings, Esmé Weijun Wang, in her recent groundbreaking work of life writing, medical inquiry, and cultural criticism, *The Collected Schizophrenias*, relays her dismay in reading about these inherent structural brain changes associated with acute and chronic schizophrenia indicative of a progressive neurological disease. "Schizophrenia's unpleasant prognosis today," Wang remarks, essentially augurs "a permanently damaged brain." After having suffered a seven-month-long psychotic episode, a symptom of schizoaffective disorder, she describes being told by her doctor that, "the longer the episode lasted, and the more frequently the episodes occurred, the more damage was occurring to my brain." This anxiety "about a loss of grey matter," she tells us, "fed a variety of delusions: one afternoon I frantically called my husband at work to babble about spiders eating holes in my brain." On the recent MRI findings she remarks, "It is disconcerting for anyone to be told that their brain is being damaged by an uncontrollable illness."[23]

Another related theory suggests that early treatment is key to staving off the damage. This view was echoed by a psychiatrist when my mother was being treated during one of her most persistent relapses, one in which she was alternately catatonic or severely delusional, unable to live on her own, being bounced between hospital psychiatric wards and the assisted living facility of Ramapo Ridge. My brother and I, realizing that my mother had endured a prolonged psychosis of several years before receiving treatment or

---

23 Wang, Esmé Weijun. *The Collected Schizophrenias: Essays.* Minneapolis, MN: Graywolf Press, 2019. 1–29.

being diagnosed with schizophrenia, lamented that if she had only received treatment sooner, perhaps the long-term neurological damage to her brain may have been significantly less.

However clarifying these medical findings might be in granting individuals with mental health disorders access to proper medical care that stresses early intervention, as well as in directing biology-based abatement of these disorders, these results that posit schizophrenia as a progressive brain disease are, for some, contentious.

Scientific studies exist that challenge these results as being the outcome of long-term use of medications or substances.

According to the authors of "The Myth of Schizophrenia as a Progressive Brain Disorder," there is much evidence to contradict the commonly held idea that schizophrenia is "a deteriorating disease, reinforced by MRI findings of progressive brain tissue loss over the early years of illness." Consumer and family groups instead find that "the majority of people with schizophrenia have the potential to achieve long-term remission and functional recovery." Recent studies take into consideration types of medication, sedentary lifestyle, duration of untreated psychosis, and stress, among other factors. The authors of "The Myth of Schizophrenia...," Robert B. Zipursky, Thomas J. Reilly, and Robin M. Murray point to "compelling evidence that antipsychotic medications have an important role in contributing to these 'progressive' [brain] changes." Remarking on the implications of many peer reviewed studies, the authors advocate that "mental health pro-fessionals need to join with patients and their families in understanding that schizophrenia is not a malignant disease that inevitably deteriorates over time, but rather one from which most people can achieve a substantial degree of recovery."[24]

Considering this view, I am reminded of how deeply perspicacious my mother remained despite the intense extrapyramidal side effects of her treatment. Despite the limitations in her coordination and the marked insecurity that abounded with everyday decisions, she remained inquisitive about the political realities of the times. She spent hours focused on her favorite MSNBC programs, paying keen attention to Barack Obama's presidency. She often advised my brother in matters related to academic achievement and advancement. At times, she dared to dabble in the buying of high-risk stocks, without the benefit of having been weaned on such capitalistic pursuits. Despite the march of time, and despite the many relapses she endured, my mother craved more intellectual engagement, and never less.

---

24 Zipursky, R., Reilly, T. and Murray, R. "The Myth of Schizophrenia as a Progressive Brain Disease." *Schizophrenia Bulletin*. 2013 Nov; 39(6): 1363–1372. Accessed 6 Nov. 2019. Web.

8

love and disappointment

Spring 2013

I continued to fight the tide of my mother's waning appetite. Shopping for her at Ralphs, I noted a sale on expensive bottled water. Fiji Water. I was reminded of my mother's dream when I was a child that she would travel to Fiji one day. A pack of ten large bottles of Fiji Water was only just over one dollar a bottle. A deal I could not resist. This water seemed the perfect solution. Since her medications had stopped working, my mother struggled to manipulate ordinary household objects. The Britta water filter she had come to rely upon for the past year was useless and she was now fastidious about drinking bottled water.

When I brought the hulking package of bottles back to her apartment, I made the worst kind of mistake, babbling on about the virtues of expensive bottled water with its vivifying electrolytes. "This is good water," I gushed somewhat anxiously. "Like Smartwater."

"I don't want electrolytes," she griped. "Take it back."

Here we stood together in her galley kitchen. Once more to protect ourselves from prying eyes, my mother had insisted the shades of her apartment be closed at all times, even though this seventh-floor apartment faced a clear view of the mountains. Everything was suspect. The water. Sunlight. Preparing food for her, too, was an exhausting enterprise. Hard to believe: only months before she had welcomed me into this kitchen, insisting I eat, doling out little treats from her refrigerator, blueberries in a bowl, delicious pitted dates. Now, nothing I did was right. I couldn't relax. After she commanded me one too many times, I snapped. I said things I had promised myself never to say. I dredged up the past. I badgered her. I told her that I was not going to put up with this abuse. I recounted the physical and verbal tirades from my childhood. In a tone as hostile as hers, I protested that I would not let her yell at or abuse me like she did when I was a child.

"Rubbish," she shouted in her defense. "I never did that."

What was behind her blunt rejection of the truth? Pride? Illness-induced memory loss? The agitation of such a prolonged psychosis? I had no definitive answer. After administering her evening pills—the Haldol, Seroquel, Cogentin, blood pressure medications, and replacement hormones—I took out the garbage and headed for my car. Parked on one of the many maddeningly identical, labyrinthine streets of the sprawling one-hundred-and-sixty-acre housing complex with mustard-painted garden apartments, almost like army barracks, and its *Prisoner*-like ambiance, it took me a few moments to orient myself. I finally found my car and maneuvered for the front gate where an uniformed guard in an anachronistic Canadian Mountie uniform negotiated the flow of traffic. It was there that I called my brother and made an agonizing request.

"Can we just stop taking care of her? Can we call 911 and let them take it from there?"

"You mean abandon her?" John responded after a thoughtful pause.

As unbelievable as it might sound, I could no longer fathom caring for my mother. I had no immediate family to rely upon for counsel or assistance other than my brother. Having blundered not getting medical help for her sooner, I found myself more and more shaken by my mother's escalating paranoid accusations.

"Yes," I responded ardently. "Abandon her."

My brother then confessed to having had similar thoughts during phases of her illness when the situation appeared to be hopeless, when after months of treatment nothing seemed to be working.

"If we do that," he spun a terrifying scenario, "she will

be bounced from hospital to hospital. And then when her Medicare runs out and the insurance won't pay for her anymore, she'll end up in an assisted living facility, where they'll drain her of all her money, and after that, when she has nothing left, she will end up on the street."

For a brief moment, driving down Third Street in rush hour traffic at twilight, I contemplated the idea of my mother homeless and fending for herself on the streets of Los Angeles. I weighed the pain of forsaking my mother with the agony of caring for her in her present state. Everywhere I turned, stationed on bus benches or maneuvering shopping carts filled haphazardly with worldly possessions, people appeared to be in a predicament similar to the one my brother described.

"I guess we can't do that," I relented, losing myself for a short time in the mounting violet of the desert night sky.

Nothing according to plan

My mother's psychiatrist had agreed that she might benefit from at-home care as opposed to being committed to a hospital. We hadn't done this on a whim. Initially we had been supported in our idea. We had been told that in approximately two weeks the drugs should start to work. Over a month had passed now, and she wasn't better. In fact, she seemed aggressively worse. After my frenzied phone call, John checked in with her doctor about our options. The doctor suggested we double up on her Haldol since we were unable to increase the Seroquel without medical supervision. John agreed to this plan, and the doctor wrote a prescription.

Of course nothing went as planned. The following day there was confusion at the pharmacy about her prescription, so we couldn't get those other pills. My brother did not want to administer the higher dosage without a written prescription from the doctor even though we were in possession of the medication. It was another week before we would be able to increase the dosage of the Haldol my mother was taking.

Parkinson's disease

Past experience told me that my mother would not want to take a higher dose of Haldol, what had been the preferred emergency psychiatric fix from the late 1960s through the early 1980s. My mother was all too aware of the negative side effects of Haldol, a dopamine inverse agonist. However my only thought at this juncture was to get her on more medication, anything in order to see some improvement.

That evening in her apartment, I tried to prepare her for the increase from five milligrams to ten.

"John spoke to your doctor, and this was his suggestion. We know you need more medication. You're not getting better," I explained, hopeful she might agree to the change. My mother became very agitated.

"No, no," she said, glancing fretfully at her hands. "I'll get Parkinson's disease."

At wit's end, I shamefully demanded that she increase her dosage of Haldol.

"I'll end my life if you don't," I said, making an unbelievable threat, and not for the first time.

Running to the safety of her bedroom, she shouted in her defense, "No, I'll get Parkinson's disease." As was so often the case, my mother was correct in her general view of her healthcare. The tremors in her body would be uncontrollable. This doctor-sanctified solution would get us nowhere.

The dopamine system

Now I had two parents in this state. The irony was not lost on me. When I turned thirty-four and moved from San Francisco to Los Angeles, shortly after publishing my fantastic novella, I noted a perceptible difference in my father's physiology. His left hand had begun to involuntarily shake. Prone to romantic viewpoints, at first I thought this was age-related or the effect of a commanding personality. My father's "tight grip" on things had translated into a nervous tic. He was advancing in years, I rationalized—in his mid-fifties. Perhaps he was simply "breaking down." No one told me otherwise, and I never bothered to ask. The denial might also have been the result of an unquestioning belief in my father's life-affirming powers. I couldn't fathom a case in which my father would experience human frailty or vulnerability. Only after a strangely prescient dream did I guess something might be wrong.

When I called to ask my father about his tremor, his wife answered the phone.

"What's wrong with Dad's hand?" I demanded. She declined to answer, remarking that it would be better if my father were to tell me. "You must tell me," I was adamant. "I have the right to know."

"Your father has Parkinson's disease," she told me, a result of his early experiments on microwave-excited electron paramagnetic resonance in rare earths. At the time, it was not widely known that continuous exposure to these elements might result in neurological disease, even death. The impact of such exposure, even today, is not completely clear.

My stepmother tried to explain to me my father's condition: "You know how your mother has too much dopamine, well, your father has too little."

While the role dopamine plays in schizophrenia is much more complex and not at all conclusive, I could not help but find my stepmother's words strangely fitting. That my parents would suffer from the same disorder, only on different ends of the neurological spectrum seemed oddly clarifying. Spartan, smart, virtually unconcerned with material things or acquisition, they shared an inexplicable affinity for as far back as I could remember. My father made a lifetime of studying the formation of stars using an instrument invisible to the naked human eye. My mother, too, appeared distracted by a realm imperceptible to most.

Closed for repairs

My mother complied with our wishes that she increase her dosage and began to visibly shake almost right away. Tremors taking hold of her legs, her hands. She sat listlessly on the couch and stared out the window, partaking in little else. She rarely spoke, had stopped eating, and refused to take walks. She fought me whenever I tried taking her to the hair salon.

"It's dirty there," she would complain. Or: "They won't want me there," she would murmur in a soft, heart-breaking tone. Just as inexplicably, she refused visits to the La Brea Park café where we once ate fruit that she liked.

"It's closed for repairs," she would say.

"It's not," I would counter, urging her to go outside.

The only time she smiled was when she was in the company of her granddaughter.

Then one night when her health aide had the day off and neither John nor I were available to help, she refused to take her pills.

Our mother's health aide, Laura, called to tell my brother the following morning.

"Your mother did not take her evening pills."

Upon hearing the bad news, immediately John left work, whisking Mom to the emergency room of Resnick Neuro-psychiatric Hospital at UCLA Medical Center, the one facility where, her doctor told us, he might have some influence.

Admittance

One of the difficulties of my mother's illness was persuading medical authorities that she was indeed sick and deserving of medical attention. Someone suffering from paranoia does not communicate perceived threats for obvious reasons. However, if it were not immediately clear that she was under the thrall of powerful hallucinations and delusions, she would not be admitted to the hospital and would be denied essential care. It is easy to become distrustful in the face of a system in which insurance companies habitually deny claims regardless of one's right to obtain treatment. Our best defense would be to claim that our mother was no longer thriving.

John explained it to me this way: "She is no longer drinking water or eating. They *have* to take her."

After my brother waited twelve-hours overnight with my mother in the light and airy emergency room with its steel and glass-vaulted ceiling, the next morning he had to leave to fulfill his teaching duties. It was my turn to become versed in the art of hospital admittances—a role I had been ducking for some time. At 11 a.m., I arrived. My mother looked agitated, her eyes wide and despairing. She was still unable to eat, rejecting food that I had brought for her, a sandwich and small Caesar salad. When her turn for admittance came, there were no beds left so we were shown to a makeshift cot in a small annex, where a security guard monitored the emergency room facilities on two separate video feeds. As if she were being slowly dispossessed of her senses, my mother snapped at whomever entered.

"What's that? ... What's going on?"

Terrified we would be sent away without proper care, I confided in the intern assigned to my mother how we ended up here.

"She was doing fine until the pharmacy gave her the wrong dosage of her meds. We were hoping she would get better on her own after a couple of weeks of taking the correct dosage," I continued but explained that she was now refusing to take her pills.

"Should she be living alone?" the young gruff intern said within earshot of my mother, folding his arms over his chest.

"Where is she supposed to live? She doesn't have the income to pay for a reasonable nursing home. She was independent for thirty years," I gushed. "She had a really good run."

I regretted my spiel immediately. How would we get a bed in this A-list facility now?

The intern in green scrubs then asked me to list my mother's delusions. I outlined for him the ones I could recall: "She thinks it's raining in her apartment when it's clearly not," I enumerated. "She says her teeth are falling out. She refuses to eat. Someone is poisoning her sandwiches. She doesn't think I'm me anymore." He shook his head. Apparently this was not strange enough.

"You will need to list *all* of her delusions for the psychiatrist," he warned in a stern voice.

I was dismayed, flummoxed. What was he hoping to hear? That she was under some kind of mind control? That she believed she was the second coming of Jesus Christ or a reincarnation of Helen Keller?

She had been under psychiatric care for over thirty years. Wasn't that proof enough?

X-ray

We were in luck. It was decided after a short physical exam that my mother was indeed having trouble. A fleshy ridge had formed under her bottom lip: a consequence of prolonged dehydration, I was informed by a nursing assistant. This ridge had appeared during her last hospitalization, and its appearance frightened me. Learning that she had been in a prolonged state of dehydration was humbling. I had been remiss not to get her medical attention sooner.

The next complaint they addressed was of a "broken hip." She told the resident about her hip being broken, of no longer being able to walk well. It was in a sense the truth: having lain in bed for a month, neglecting to eat, she had lost much of her coordination. Even though I told the doctors that I believed the broken hip was a delusion, the medical doctors wanted to check to be sure there was not an actual problem with her hip replacement. At first, my mother rejected taking an x-ray, proclaiming a fear of radiation poisoning. But once she had become acclimated to her healthcare specialists, she gave in to their request.

I was beginning to get a clearer view of her illness. She needed time to adjust to her surroundings and gentle engagement in order to establish trust. The results of her x-ray confirmed that she had not fractured or broken anything and served to put an end to her attachment to this belief.

Another week passes

My brother's return to the hospital was perfectly timed. An exceedingly helpful female psychiatrist had just finished examining our mother. She did not query us or demand proof of my mother's illness.

"I have both good and bad news," she said, leaning against the open doorway of the annex where we had spent a good part of the day. The good news was that she had just spoken with my mother's psychiatrist who had returned her phone call on a Friday night, detailing our mother's needs in full.

"That's a first," my brother noted, delighted a doctor had advocated for our mother for a change. The bad news was that there were no beds. We would have to take our mother home, then call first thing Monday morning to get on the waiting list. This being Friday evening, there would be no more discharges from the hospital until the beginning of the week. We had waited nearly twelve hours in the emergency ward for this disheartening news.

After a worrying weekend, on Monday my brother called the number he was given in the emergency room only to learn that there was no actual "waiting list." The conditions for becoming a lucky recipient of a bed were nebulous, perhaps predicated on one's insurance and ability to pay. A week passed before my mother gained admittance to the famed neuropsychiatric facility, with its seventy-four inpatient beds. A staggeringly small number given that "one out of every twenty-four [California residents] have a mental illness so serious it becomes difficult for them to function in daily life."[25]

"There is only one small problem," my brother alerted me. "They have placed Mom in the eating disorder ward." Apparently there was no space in the general psychiatric ward, and given my mother's inability to eat, that she should end up here seemed strangely fitting. "But these rooms are huge," he relayed over the phone. "She has a couch and an enormous bathroom."

25 Weiner, Jocelyn. "Breakdown: California's Mental Health System, Explained." *CalMatters*, 30 Apr. 2019. Web.

The following day

After parking in the hospital's pricey underground parking lot, it took me some time to reach my mother's ward. I traveled on various elevators to the fourth floor, traversing some distance through long dreary corridors before I finally managed to find the correct security door and was shown to my mother's room. From my brother's depiction, I expected something more regal. The room was big but drab; though I could hardly complain. There was a hard-looking vinyl couch. The floor was laid with dreary, institutional tile. However the main drawback was the room's view. My mother's room did not look out upon gardens, green spaces, or gathering areas like the hospital literature touted. Above the couch, a large window looked out onto a beige-painted rooftop occupied by a vast mechanical and electrical system.

I found my mother seated upright on her bed dressed in the powder-blue button-down sweater I had recently bought her and a pair of baggy pants. Seated beside her was a pretty young nurse's aide. She explained to me that at first, my mother didn't want me to visit.

"She didn't think she looked good enough," her aide said. "But then she let me help her get dressed and brush her hair."

I was proud of my mother for overcoming her anxieties. She seemed more at peace here. Mom smiled at me and lowered her head for a kiss. But once her nurse's aide had left, the problems began to announce themselves.

"I have nothing to wear," she alerted me.

"You do. Mom, look." I found most of what she needed in a built-in cubby area. Several T-shirts, some pants. Underwear. She then cast a frightened glance toward the window and the view of the massive equipment and its billowing steam.

"Look," she noted in a hushed voice. "It's raining." I didn't have much patience for her worries and diverted her attention, suggesting we take a walk.

Alas, in this bite-sized ward there was just about nowhere to go. The crescent-shaped hallway that facilitated the flow of patients extended no more than ten yards in either direction. I would soon learn that the eating disorder patients, mostly young women and rail thin, were discouraged from partaking in much exercise. Days were spent moving languidly back and forth between the spacious private rooms and the common room, where they worked on uncompetitive games like puzzles or busied themselves with paint-by-number kits, watched television, often times hooked up to a mobile IV. It was a quiet, intimate ward with no more than seven patients at any one time.

Our ambitions for a walk now over, I focused instead on ordering my mother meals from a select and enticing menu, little of which would get eaten.

Noisy wards

After a worrying weekend, on Monday, as promised, Mom was moved from the eating disorder ward to the appropriate facility. The setting was noisier. The rooms were smaller, the hallways longer. There were more patients, more beds. In this environment my mother's calm demeanor faded. Immediately she grew angrier and more suspicious. When I first arrived, I found her in bed lying prone at a strange angle. She complained especially of the noise. Sensitivity to sound is often linked to schizophrenia. This took a visible toll on my mother. I was also alarmed to find her in a hospital gown that was thoughtlessly open, exposing her belly in a needless way. Did her male nurse's aid not notice? On edge, I found myself making everything much worse, complaining about my mother's attire. Eventually my mother's psychiatrist appeared: a soft-spoken man in his mid-fifties, whose sallow complexion made his admirable commitment to his work abundantly clear.

His first suggestion was that we reduce the amount of Haldol she was on: "You can see she is already beginning to suffer from a Parkinsonian-like dystonia." The medication had only worsened her condition, he explained. My mother's fears had been justified. He suggested we lower it back to five milligrams.

"He's not very smart," my mother confided in me when he left the room, the same complaint she had about her doctor at Ramapo Ridge. I was beginning to see a pattern.

Medicare days

My mother continued to have difficulty eating. We had been asked by the medical staff to bring any special foods she might enjoy. But nothing compared with what was on offer at Resnick. I was bowled over by the ample portions of grilled salmon, chicken, seasoned rice. These meals were not inexpensive. Dubious I could do any better, I tried tempting my mother with lovely stews, salmon, and rice dishes bought at a neighboring gourmet store. Nothing stirred her appetite. I used more space in the communal refrigerator than was our right, stocking up on high-protein yogurts.

I called her nurses daily to monitor her eating. "Please make sure she eats something. She won't get better unless she eats."

Soon my mother complained of terrible constipation. She required an enema. Throughout the painful procedure my mother moaned loudly, accusing the medical staff of purposely trying to hurt her. I grew terribly impatient with her. No one on staff, however, appeared the least bit disturbed by her behavior. This was a gift I could not offer my mother. Whether we had Medicare days left or not, observing the courteous and efficient behavior of the psychiatric staff, I vowed never to forgo proper medical care for my mother again.

The specter of our mother's dwindling Medicare days was soon to be raised again.

"Your mother cannot stay in the psychiatric facility for more than two weeks," her doctor told us. "If she needs more care, you might be able to get her signed in as a medical patient of Ronald Reagan for physical therapy."

"She will need more care than that," my brother said, reminding the doctor that she had spent three months at Ramapo Ridge before being released.

"That was far too long," our mother's doctor shook his head in disbelief. "I think she will be much better in two weeks."

John then shared his mounting fears with the doctor that at some point the medication would stop working, and she would have to endure her most acute symptoms without the relief her cocktail had afforded her for the past three decades.

"There is no reason to worry," the world-renowned doctor said to my brother. "If the medication worked before, it will continue to work."

Our fears were assuaged—we no longer needed to divvy out Medicare days to our mother with punishing paucity. We would be okay.

Two weeks after my mother's admittance to Resnick, we were told she was well enough to be released. She was still unable to care for herself, had eaten next-to-nothing in the hospital, and was still weak. We had no choice but to procure more help. Again, I was plagued with doubts that we would find someone up to the task. Her phobias and intense food aversions were hard on everyone. Luckily, my brother found someone willing to put up with our mother's difficulties. Another young Filipina immigrant, this time in her late twenties, Kate exhibited great understanding and patience toward our mother regardless of her marked troubles, including the constant complaint of persistent hip pain and an inability to walk.

Returning home, she still insisted that her television programs, the loud political fare found on MSNBC that saw her through long and lonely days, had been "vanished" by an undisclosed power. Despite Mom's delusions, despite her constant criticisms and complaints, Kate never seemed taxed. She was vigilant about taking our mother on walks unlike her previous health aide, who generally caved.

Two weeks post-release, while we had been assured of my mother's recovery, it felt far from certain. On afternoon visits, I would often find my mother seated at the table, staring fixedly into the middle distance, impervious to the scintillating view out of her casement windows. Laconic and suffering from avolition, my mother exhibited the all-too-familiar symptoms of her previous relapse.

The loss of affect and the compromised hearing were much the same. Whenever I broke into her reverie she would respond with a loud distracted, "*Hmmm*?"

The end of the line

In the dream, I am standing at the edge of an elevated platform of the historic Chatham, New Jersey station waiting for a train. I have no recollection of being here before. The perimeter of this rail line is leafy and green, bordered by mature mulberry trees. The earth is pungent and rich, perfumed with the smells of late spring or early summer.

I patiently wait for the train, peering down the tracks for the slow appearance of the locomotive engine, just as I once did in high school waiting for the Erie Lackawanna. As I stand waiting anxiously for a train which never appears, studying the rusting ties that lie across slate-colored gravel, slowly the station goes out of existence, bit by bit like the dissolution of the soda-drink stand in a Philip K. Dick novel. The gravel. Rusting metal ties. The dividing metal fence. Green storybook red-tiled roof station house. I am confounded, left alone to wait on a sliver of disappearing sidewalk for no reason I can think of.

A daily spoonful

Over the next few weeks, my mother's complaints about daily life only intensified. She couldn't go to CVS with Kate anymore because her aide was a "kleptomaniac." She insisted after a pedicure that she could no longer walk across her carpet because her feet "had lost their grip."

Teaching an intensive workshop at SCI-Arc that summer, I was not able to ensure that she was eating during the day.

"The medication doesn't work without food," I reminded my mother whenever we spoke on the phone. She was still insisting most foods were too hard. Bread crusts, crackers, and fruit bars were all too challenging; she consumed only the most judicious amounts of yogurt per day. A visit to the dentist did nothing to alter her view. Whenever I asked if she had taken her Ensure, she answered in the affirmative, but the desultory quality of her voice told me otherwise.

I was beginning to grow weary of a situation I could not change. Eventually my promises of stopping by went unfulfilled. Finally, I decided that I would only stop by when I could be joined by my brother and niece. Determined to shield her granddaughter from her illness, this was when my mother was on her best behavior.

Strawberries and cream

One Saturday afternoon in May, I met my brother and niece at my mother's apartment for lunch. Shortly after my brother finished helping my mother with her bills, we took the elevator down to the lobby for our routine weekly walk. Behind her apartment complex we traversed the sandy pathway circling the large picturesque grounds with its majestic date palms, flowering purple jacarandas, stunning drought resistant plants, and radiant bougainvillea. Compromised and weak, our mother in a white sun hat and matching cropped white pants lagged somewhat behind. We were perhaps not as patient with our mother as we should have been.

"Come on, Joy," I kept calling back to her. She seemed out of breath and a little flustered by the end of our walk.

Afterward, we piled into my brother's car and headed for our favorite inexpensive Chinese restaurant located on Beverly Boulevard. We ordered our dishes of deep-fried shrimp in a delicious, incongruous sauce of strawberries and cream, as well as a plate of ginger chicken, and green beans. During this outing my brother succeeded in getting my mother to eat a healthy portion of her meal.

"See," he said, heaping her plate with a second helping of rice. "She's getting better."

Her appetite had visibly improved. The complaints about her teeth had significantly subsided. I began to feel hopeful again.

The Story of Joy

Mid-June. Under a marine layer offering much-needed protection from the ceaseless sun, I drove my regular route to Park La Brea along Third Street, taking in the reassuring and familiar sites of Hancock Park: the two-story, large fabled homes of early Hollywood celebrities with their leafy trees and bushes, tall imposing walls and now, a preponderance of Orthodox Jewish women attired in expensive fashionable knee-length dresses and high heels, guiding strollers past cafes or glitzy clothing stores. Six weeks after my mother's release, my mother's doctor began to reduce the heavy dosage of Seroquel our mother was taking: from the fog-inducing five hundred milligrams to four hundred milligrams. Her improvement was immediate. Less confused and more motivated, my mother began to make requests for specific food items. We became convinced that she was ready to live on her own again.

With her continued improvement, my interest in her medical history grew. By this time, I had begun openly writing about my mother's illness after a lifetime of silence. Not having participated in my mother's healthcare for many years, I asked John to fill me in. We arranged to meet one evening to take our mother to a nearby restaurant. As I recall, it took an especially long time to persuade her to leave the apartment; she seemed both agitated and weary. We drove the short distance, two long city blocks. Struggling to find new and affordable places to take our mother, we knew at least this barbeque house with its 1950s retro furnishings and dark wood paneling would be to her liking.

My brother ordered my mother a healthy dish of salmon and rice and beans, skillfully thwarting her attempts to order the lowest calorie meal on the menu, a diet-conscious salad. Some argument ensued. Despite this, my mother was successful in eating most of it. She had turned a corner, just as my brother had assured me she would. The plan for this evening was to interview my brother after dinner, but by the time we finished eating, I could feel my energy waning. No longer able to curb my impatience, I slipped into interview mode as my mother headed for the bathroom. Catching me on my laptop upon her return, she soon registered what was happening, tuning in to my brother's depiction of a prior relapse.

I expected my mother to recoil angrily, rankled by the open discussion of her illness. Instead she was eager to participate.

"No," she corrected my brother's memory of the ill-fated change in her medication by her doctor those fifteen-odd years ago. "He had me on fifteen milligrams of Haldol, and he reduced it by five milligrams." I was impressed by her fine recall of facts.

In the low lighting of this bustling restaurant, our discussion of her multiple hospitalizations continued. My mother participated without rancor or confusion.

"You're not writing about me?" she asked, an excited gleam in her eye.

"No, I'm not," I dissembled, afraid of my mother's censure.

"You *are*," she countered with notable relish.

"Okay, Mom, I admit it," masking my intent with a heavy dollop of irony. "I'm going to title the book: *The Story of Joy*," I said with an extra flourish.

My brother nudged me. "I like that," he said in all sincerity.

"That's a terrible title," I groused.

Across the table from us, despite my heresy, our mother continued to beam.

Delusion of reference

Still the delusions persisted. When it came time to pay, she placed her credit card on the table with the following complaint:

"This card is not my credit card. It has silver patterns on it," she said, pointing to its identifying hologram. "My card didn't have patterns."

Described in medical terms as "a delusion of reference," as in the case of her telephone, nothing actually belonged to her anymore. It wasn't uncommon for her to insist that the phone she was speaking to me on belonged to a mysterious "them."

She continued to insist the newly issued credit card in her wallet was not hers. My brother did his best to make light of her complaints, parodying her distinctive southern-African accent.

"I don't like this card," he mocked in a high-pitched voice, tossing his hands in the air in a display of helpless femininity. "It's not mine."

My mother began to laugh. This was a familiar tack on the part of my brother. Identifying closely with a maddening effect of her disorder, he helped her find some detachment. To laugh at herself and move on. I had never comprehended my brother's grating parodies of my mother's accent before. Now I understood this strategy's power.

It wasn't long, however, before she launched into another round of delusions.

"I can't eat in my kitchen," she complained to us as we rose in our seats to leave the restaurant. "There are rats scurrying up and down the walls." The bright gleam in her eyes told us she knew this was a symptom of her illness.

"Fine, Mom," my brother jibed. "We'll buy you a pet rat if that's what you want." Again she giggled, glad to be in on the joke. My brother's disarming comments worked to curtail the familiar litany of gothic horrors. Once again, I had to wonder why my mother suffered from hallucinations that were strictly terrifying. Why did her mind never manufacture something beneficent or at the very least benign? That night, dropping off our mother at her apartment, she seemed especially sad to see us go.

Mid-summer with scorching triple-digit temperatures, teaching writing to art students at UC Irvine, I was now commuting along congested freeways under interminably sunny skies. Conscious of the vulnerability of the elderly during heat waves, I became worried about my mother. Would she even know to turn on the air conditioner? She lived on the seventh floor of a tower building. I could only imagine how hot it would get. Stuck in the slow crawl of rush-hour traffic on the freeway, I called from the car.

"It's over a hundred degrees today. Turn on your air conditioner," I insisted. She refused.

"It's too loud. I can't." I felt confused. I had never noticed the air conditioner in her apartment being loud. I was over sixty miles away. I couldn't easily reach her.

At 6 p.m. when I returned home, I noted a cooling ocean breeze had reduced temperatures significantly. I called my mother to suggest she open her windows to get some fresh air.

"I can't," she told me. "They are drilling outside the apartment day and night. From 8 a.m. until 8 p.m."

"I didn't know that," I responded, unsure what to believe.

"Any day now, they will come and demolish my building."

"I don't think so," I countered. It had been years since I had heard this particular fear. She then added a nightmarish confession: "I am the only person living here."

I tried reminding her that we saw people getting in and out of both of the towers's elevators all of the time.

"No," she refused my version of reality. Other false beliefs had become more persistent as well. She informed me of a complicated scenario in which electronic signals were being relayed between the downstairs security office and her neighbor's apartment, and how these signals interfered with the use of her phone and the television. There were references too, to men who purportedly showed up and did things in her apartment that she refused to divulge.

"Why don't I ever see one of these men?" I asked.

"They only come when you're not here," she said in full command of her imaginary world. Dismayed that she seemed altogether worse than the week before, I ended the conversation.

Capgras delusion

Soon I would be confronted with a familiar accusation.

Opening her front door to greet me one day, she declared, "I don't think you are Claire."

My brother and I had not heard this delusion in over thirty years. This was a symptom of Capgras delusion or syndrome, a psychiatric disorder in which a close relative, friend, or even doctor, is deemed an imposter, first described in 1923 by Capgras and Reboul-Lachax. Its reemergence gave me the impression that this illness, left unabated, followed a specific neurological course. Researching this particular syndrome, I found that, according to psychiatrist Dr. Sadgun Bhandari, these "delusions of misidentification are common in late onset delusions both with and without cognitive impairment. A related phenomenon is that of phantom boarder syndrome in which patients believe their home is inhabited by un-welcome guests."[26]

26 Bhandari, Sadgun. "Descriptive psychopathology." *Core Psychiatry* (Third Edition) Eds. Pádraig Wright, Julian Stern, and Michael Phelan. Philadelphia: W.B. Saunders, 2012. 83–93.

This could explain why she had been insisting for months that her telephone did not belong to her. It was an imposter phone. Just like Phillip K. Dick's imposter police station in his science fiction classic *Do Androids Dream of Electric Sheep?*, where bounty hunter Rick Deckard of a future dystopic San Francisco hunts down android escapees of Mars. It also explained why she insisted on the constant presence of invisible intruders.

This delusion carried some unwholesome effects. For instance, when it came to her healthcare, she refused to see her doctor or make a dental appointment, insisting either: *He won't be there* or *It won't be him*. If she were to reach her doctor, she was convinced it would only be to speak to an imposter.

The imposter syndrome signaled to me that her psychosis had been running on for way too long.

Mother and daughter

"Why don't you get your hair done?" I suggested to my mother later that week. She didn't wash her hair, having relied on professional care as far back as I could remember. These appointments were vital to her personal hygiene.

"I can't go because my hair is falling out," she countered. I wasn't sure if this was a delusion or an effect of her poor eating over the past several months.

"Let's make an appointment," I would suggest to her.

"I can't," she refused, returning to a litany of former complaints. "They won't want me there. It's dirty."

Scoping about her apartment, hoping to help, I reminded

her to try and start taking her vitamins again. Before her relapse, my mother was markedly disciplined about her health. She took scads of daily vitamins: special supplements for eyes, skin, bones, so many I couldn't keep up with them all. Now, her vitamins languished in the bottles and the weekly prescription dispensers, her woefully underpaid health aides had filled for her as part of their duties.

"Mom, take your vitamins," I begged.

"I can't take my vitamins," she explained in a weakened voice. "They smell bad, and half are missing."

I began to fear a recovery might never be possible.

Caregiving

Some days were better than others. In a crusade to gain weight, my mother had taken herself to the Cheesecake Factory for a slice of her favorite dessert. The good news ended here.

"There was blood in my milkshake today," she confided. "I couldn't finish it."

My heart sank. What chance did my mother have to thrive if she believed her food was contaminated? How could I convince her otherwise? It was impossible. Throughout the night, anxious and sleepless, I sent my brother a slew of panicked emails. "Mom is not getting better. She can't take care of herself, and I am drowning in course work. She needs to be placed in a home."

"A psychiatric home would cost us $9,000 a month," my brother informed me the following day. We simply didn't have the money. Her insurance would not cover psychiatric care of this type. My brother insisted he had been through this with her multiple times, watching her undergo dramatic weight loss under the sway of pernicious delusions before responding suddenly to a new medication and recovering. "A home would bankrupt her in a matter of months," he told me. "She's improving, Claire. It's slow. But she is getting better. Her delusions are tapering off. Mom will live another twenty years."

"But how can she survive when she thinks there is blood in her food?" I raised the specter of the milkshake story.

"You need to understand, she's always lived with delusions. She's eating entire meals whenever I take her out. She always tells me how hungry she is. She's taking long walks now. She's able to put her bills out for me now. Last month she couldn't even do that. Please." He tried schooling me in her care. "You need to give her more time." He advised me to take a break. "A friend once told me, you should always stop taking care of other people if it begins to interfere with your ability to take care of yourself."

Promising to see more of her, my brother gave me a reprieve. It was time for me to step away. Get some rest. Mark some papers.

For about two to three days, I stopped calling. It didn't seem reasonable to call when my attitude was so overtly unsympathetic. I was worried about her though. So, soon afterward I started up again. I wondered how she coped alone at night with all of those alarming delusions. I needed to hear her voice. Contrary to my fears, my mother was perfectly capable of staying out of trouble. She didn't abandon her apartment for another one, wander naked throughout the halls of her apartment building, or go missing.

That Friday, having taken my architecture students to a see an exhibit of models and blueprints, renderings, and hand drawings at the Architecture & Design Museum, *Never Built L.A. Architecture*, and after reviewing several unrealized proposals, including Rem Koolhaas's irreverent bid to tent LACMA and its disparate stew of buildings, I left, intending to surprise my mother with a quick unannounced visit.

Her green eyes flickered as she opened the door of her sun-flooded apartment, delighted to see me. I found her busy folding laundry. Apparently, she had convinced my brother that she no longer needed a health aide. She appeared thin but kempt in her white cotton peasant blouse and exercise pants, and surer on her feet. Checking on her progress, I opened the refrigerator. It was almost bare. I became frantic.

"There's no food. You're not eating. You need help," I implored. I then scanned her kitchen for more proof of her need of part-time help. "Why are there so many unclean dishes in your sink?"

"A man was here working on the plumbing," she said in possession of herself. "I am not paying rent until they fix a problem with the plumbing."

I was confused. I saw no signs of work, or a man.

"I don't believe there was a man," I chided. How many times over the past several months had I heard about these mysterious "others?" Noting the dingy carpet of her living room, I then asked her how she would get by without any help. "You need a new health aide. You can't do all of this alone. No one has cleaned these floors in weeks."

"I do have help," Mom boasted happily. "Clara was supposed to be here at noon. But she didn't come."

"Really? Where did you meet Clara?" I asked incredulous.

"I met her doing laundry. She had a big ring in her nose," my mother chuckled, gesturing to her face. "She showed me how to get my whites clean."

Apparently, Clara was helping another woman in the building with her household chores, and was kind enough to explain to my mother how to separate her clothes in order to keep the whites bright. Wow—for how long had my mother labored without that bit of domestic knowledge? The interaction sounded credible, though I still held some reservations, mainly because Clara's name was uncannily so close to my own.

Just then, the doorbell rang. My mother and I exchanged surprised looks. Who could this be? I opened the door to a young woman, Clara, who, as described, sported a hulking septum nose ring. My mother hadn't dreamed up Clara. Here she was, just two hours late. She was only eighteen. What could we expect? My mother and I shared a laugh over Clara's late arrival and my recalcitrant disbelief.

"Do you want to work today?" I asked. Clara answered in the affirmative. As I had done for a number of health aides over the past nine months, I demonstrated for her my mother's daily regime. Her particular habits about emptying the trash, cleaning the bathroom, the kitchen floor, then negotiated an hourly rate for her of $12. She seemed amenable to this arrangement. Her timing couldn't have been better. I handed her the broom and left.

Driving home, I marveled at my mother's resourcefulness. She hadn't waited for my brother to hire someone new. She had found someone on her own, a delightful young woman who was planning on enrolling at El Camino College in the Fall. It felt fated, almost magical.

Gunned down

Suddenly, we were back to where we started. My mother had succumbed to yet another debilitating round of diarrhea. For two days, she complained to me about her symptoms over the phone. There had been another Foster Farms chicken salmonella outbreak, I would discover later. Was this the culprit? I wasn't sure. Not willing to face another hospitalization, I begged her to call her doctor, or call 911, or go directly to the emergency room. She consistently refused. Too paranoid to make the call to her doctor, she insisted that if she did, an imposter would be there in his place.

"It won't be him," she said.

Luckily my brother was willing to intervene, making the visit to her home, as I madly dashed great distances between colleges in bright, sickening heat. She was legitimately ill, I soon learned, a reality I still struggled to embrace. I had never suffered from food poisoning, or from a bacteria outbreak or food-borne illness. Ensconced in my bubble of wellness, I could not relate. My brother then made a worse discovery. She was now no longer taking her pills.

"You are not someone who gets to choose whether you take your medication. You must always take your pills," he tried coaxing her into self-care. My mother could not have been more fortunate in begetting this son who proved to be, more often than not, patient and undaunted in the face of chronic illness and its many demands.

Just as she had claimed, she had suffered a terrible bout of diarrhea and was in need of care. Her linens were soiled. She needed help with bathing. Not only that, but under the influence of a persistent psychosis, she was convinced that she had been gunned down.

"I've been shot," she kept insisting as my brother worked to dutifully wash her, confusing the unpleasant discharge with an unthinkable amount of blood.

Cedars-Sinai

My mother and I hadn't been getting along well for some time. Burned out on hospitals—and frankly, phobic—I didn't go see her at Cedars-Sinai. The tension in our relationship was evident by her greeting on the phone. If we were getting along I would receive the following salutation: *Hi, darling.* When we were not, when I had caused her distress with my vociferous demands, I was the recipient of a clipped: *Hi.* The "darling" pointedly elided from her greeting.

On this particular afternoon when I called her at Cedars, I received the truncated *Hi.* She was angry with me for my obvious lack of compassion about the diarrhea that had landed her in the hospital, and I couldn't blame her.

She then launched into a litany of complaints about the hospital staff and the terrible treatment she received. Once again, I was incredulous. Vivid memories of her past accusatory behavior at Ramapo Ridge came to mind. Was she at it again, ascribing paranoid motivations to the staff? I didn't call again for another two days.

"Hi, darling," she answered. I was forgiven and relieved to be in her good graces again. I missed these two simple words. I had come to count on them much more than I realized. "I love you, Claire," she said then, apropos of nothing. "Just remember that."

Voices

Continuing to read up on schizophrenia, I began to wonder if my mother ever heard voices.

"Mom," I asked during one of our nightly calls. "Do you ever hear voices?"

"No," she quipped. "Just yours."

In a better world

In Mikal Gilmore's searing, heart-rending memoir, *Shot in the Heart*, he tells a tale of family misery that recounts both his mother's disturbingly haunted Mormon past and his father's equally mysterious life as a con artist and cruel patrician, whose violent beatings of Gilmore's three significantly older brothers destroyed any hope for a united family. The most notable and violent brother, Gary, gained notoriety for having robbed and killed two men in Utah over the course of consecutive nights. Once apprehended and imprisoned, Gary demanded that he be put to death by firing squad, a shocking and violent request based on Mormon traditions that would usher back the death penalty in the United States after a ten-year hiatus.

A nationally recognized former music critic for the *L.A. Weekly*, Gilmore contemplates in his memoir the misery of being born of two people whose lives should have never been entangled: whose interwoven fates resulted in dreadful consequences. After endless beatings by his father, Gary became a juvenile delinquent, whose recidivist tendencies and struggle to remain on the "outside" effectively ended the day he shot those two Mormons dead. Gilmore includes at the end of this haunting and evocative memoir a proclamation of love for his long-since-deceased mother and father, whose affronts toward one another and their children were at times nothing short of monstrous.

"I love my parents," he writes. "These days I miss them both terribly. But there is something ironic that I have had to recognize about my act of contemplating my own family: In a better world, my parents would not have met—or at least they would not have married and had a family. In a better world, I would never have been born."

For some time after reading this passage, I felt the strong pull of these words. *In a better world, I would never have been born.*

A pleasant day

The day of her release, my brother kindly escorted Mom home from the hospital. He purchased food for her and hired a new health aide. He told me that she had been treated terribly in the hospital, her room was awful, and that she had been left to languish without care for days. Her complaints were real. Once again, I felt ashamed that I had chosen not to believe her. Shortly after her return home, I dropped by between classes to help her with laundry, as she told me that no one had done any for her for some time. When I arrived, she was seated on the floor before a clean pile of folded clothes stacked on her couch.

"These clothes are clean," I shouted, irate.

"No, they're not," she insisted, picking up one after another article of clothing, holding it to her nose and sniffing. "They smell."

What ensued was painful. It was clear to me the piles of clothes were recently washed. I couldn't accept that she was not going to get better. Mom ran from the room and collapsed onto her bed, begging me not to complain. We continued to fight that afternoon. Over the laundry. Over the money I believed she owed me for buying groceries last time I visited. After a time, I collected myself and offered to get groceries for her. When I returned, we sat down at her white pedestal kitchen table, the Santa Monica Mountains and the glittering tops of residential date palm trees in plain view out the bank of steel casement windows.

It was a pleasant day. I liked being with my mother. I registered this despite the rancor I felt that afternoon. If only I had told her so.

Low blood pressure

The following week, frail and lightheaded, she had continual falls. What I feared most became reality. After her first fall, the paramedics were called. She was taken to the hospital where she was given a battery of tests. After a few hours, they sent her home. Her blood pressure was dangerously low. No one seemed to know why. The news confused us. My mother took medication for high blood pressure. Why then did she have low blood pressure?

I continued to commute between colleges in the unremitting heat, for hours each day, allowing my brother to handle the nitty-gritty of my mother's medical care. At this stage, I felt stricken that we were holding my mother prisoner in her apartment, our private source of shame and despair, much the same as Rochester held his first wife in the attic of *Jane Eyre*. What did I fear so much? I knew she wouldn't commit suicide, or set an angry conflagration to the place, or harm anyone in any way.

What I feared was her imminent departure and potentially grisly death. I could not abide the loss of my mother, the heartbreaking sight of her inert, lifeless body. I dreaded becoming witness to those last bitter moments. Even more, perhaps, I dreaded the unhappy confrontation with having failed her that her imminent departure would inevitably confirm.

Nine lives

My attention had turned elsewhere. Shortly after my mother's first fall during the latest extreme heat wave—one that would go down as one of the hottest on record—my outdoor cat of thirteen years went missing only to appear two days later with an injured hind leg, unable to walk. This wily, semi-feral black cat, Quimby, who had survived numerous catfights, surgeries, and multiple coyote sightings, had expended another life. That Sunday at the suggestion of a friend, I whisked him to the VCA, an expensive animal hospital on the Westside. Shortly after an examination, I learned from the technician that my cat might have a torn knee ligament and would require an expensive operation.

"Operation?" I balked.

"We will know once we do the x-rays," she said. I had torn my knee ligament and not had surgery. There was no chance I was paying for Quimby's expensive knee surgery, and so I bolted.

Over the next few days, I consulted with several cat owners. *Get the operation and cage him,* was the advice. What? This sounded impossible. I lived in a small apartment. Where was I going to put this cage for the required six weeks? How would a cat used to roaming the hillsides, venturing into neighbor's homes at all times of day, deal with being caged? A local vet understood my cat's needs.

"You will never keep this breed of cat inside for more than

two weeks," she said, petting my injured black cat as she sat cross-legged on the floor of her exam room.

I was relieved. Few understood the utter misery of trying to keep a semi-feral cat indoors for any length of time. After x-raying Quimby, she advised me not to get the surgery, a $5000 ordeal, with only a fifty percent success rate.

Instead, I cared diligently for my cat with the aid of powerful pain medication, filling my mother in on my pet's wellbeing by phone. No one else in the family showed much interest.

My mother, on the other hand, listened patiently, continually checking in with me. Never once faulting me for placing my cat's care above hers.

"How's Quimby?" she would ask whenever she called.

Yummy.com

The week progressed, and I came to see my pet's debilitating injury as an augur of sorts. My mother would endure another fall upon waking. This time when the paramedics came, they did not whisk her away to the hospital. They tested her in the ambulance, determining that she was not in need of any medical attention, before bringing her straight back up to her apartment. It was the start of a new Fall semester; I had only the weekend to prep for a new course I was teaching: "Eco Writing: Green is the New Red." In the course description I had referenced Henry David Thoreau's activist line: "Let your life be a counter friction to stop the machine."

I felt a particular urgency to reacquaint myself with the material that my students at CalArts and I would be reading together, feeling somewhat estranged from nature, my days spent flitting about the congested freeways of metropolitan Southern California. Only when I reminded myself that I had once trekked the three-day Inca trail to Machu Picchu did I feel like I had anything to add on the subject of nature and the sublime. Late Friday afternoon, I called my mother after work, too tired to confront rush-hour traffic to make a trip to her apartment.

"I promise to come by tomorrow morning and bring you groceries." I said.

"Okay, darling. Not to worry. I can always order from yummy.com." We shared a laugh. My mother often complained that "yummy.com" was not very yummy.

I then commented on her recent dizzy spell: "I'm really worried about you, Mom. I'm really worried."

"Don't be," she reassured me. "I'll be fine."

At 6 p.m. it was still almost one hundred degrees. The desert sun is hottest at the end of the day. I knew my mother didn't take much interest in staying cool.

"Turn on your air conditioner," I advised, knowing something had to be wrong. Again she told me not to worry.

I went later that night to meet an out-of-town friend for a drink on Sunset Boulevard. Inconsolable after a couple of whiskey drinks, I must have had a sense of what was to come.

The next morning, seated in my small living room, a heap of books on the subject of environmental activism and nature stacked before me, I panicked. Once again, I was ready to put off spending time with my mother in order to do some work. I picked up the phone and dialed, anticipating a response from her that would be full of understanding. Instead, after an excessive number of rings, a strange man answered the phone.

"Who are you?" I assailed. "What are you doing answering my mother's phone?" In my heart of heart's I knew.

After a pause, the deep, compelling voice came back on: "Can you come to your mother's home?"

"Why?" I snapped. "Who are you?"

Again there was a measured silence, a clear reluctance to answer. "I don't want to tell you over the phone," he articulated in a voice so distinct, I can still conjure it to this day.

Slipping from my chair to the hard floor, horrified, I confessed shakily, "I can't come there alone—I need a friend."

Overcome, I called a close friend, Melanie, whose mother suffered from a similar illness. In Hollywood at her friend's private gym, she offered to come right over.

Twenty minutes passed, and Melanie arrived at my door with a bottle of cheap champagne in hand. It was not even noon. I appreciated the gesture—but I was far too disturbed to open a bottle of champagne. Sputtering along Virgil Ave., past the low-slung stucco houses in Melanie's convertible 1970s VW bug, we headed in the direction of my mother's apartment, my grief and guilt pouring out.

"Why didn't I visit her yesterday? What was I thinking?"

"Considering everything she had been through, she lived

for such a long time," Melanie reassured me, touching my knee. "She did incredibly well."

No one understood better the pain of seeing a loved one suffer than Melanie, whose mother had been over- and under-medicated with more or less the same regularity as my mother had been. Melanie knew all too well the toll and jeopardy involved in treatment. As she navigated L.A.'s congested Third Street that Saturday, I texted my brother paranoid messages, panicked that we would be found at fault for our mother's untimely end.

The endless and shadowless hereafter

"What if they accuse us of neglecting our mother? Of killing her?" I texted in a state of mild panic.

"Try not to give into your worst fears," my brother responded. "We did nothing wrong. They should have admitted her into the hospital instead of sending her home."

I arrived at my mother's apartment to find two policemen and her health aide milling about the living room. Someone must have told me that my mother was located in the bedroom, after which the Latino officer interrogated me on the subject of my mother's medication.

"Why was she taking so many pills?" the officer asked.

"She suffered from schizophrenia," I said. "They had her on a lot of medication. She had had a hysterectomy," I continued, explaining away the hormone replacement pills. Seroquel. Haldol. Thyroid pills. Hormones. Cogentin. Zoloft. The list went on. Once I had detailed our mother's medical history— the blood pressure, thyroid problem, mental illness—any further line of inquiry was dropped.

I was not to blame. All this while a health aide sat in the far corner of the living room, one I had not met before. In fact, I was not even aware that a new aide had been hired, and was relieved to know that at least she had not been alone in her final hour. Subdued, she was an older woman, perhaps not that much younger than my mother. I felt for this woman working for minimum pay and who had the misfortune of being on duty during this difficult moment. I hoped she did not blame herself and said something to this effect.

By the time my brother arrived, Melanie had already left. Pale and frantic, John dashed into the bright clean kitchen to take a moment for himself.

"This should not have happened," he said in a shaken undertone. "She should not have died."

Returning to the large living room, he asked for the details.

I did not want to hear them and clasped my hands to my ears. Fully aware that a good writer, an ambitious one, would have been eager to hear what happened, might have stepped into her bedroom to view her body, to face her death, I found myself paralyzed and unable to confront my mother's lifeless body.

One of the L.A.P.D. officers took the lead in explaining to us that she had had a heart attack. The same officer whose voice it was on my mother's phone and who would confide in me later, while flirting with me, the perils of a difficult job, his former use of alcohol and drugs in coping. He turned to my mother's health aide to fill in the picture.

She told us that our mother had gotten up from bed that morning and once again, like she had earlier that week, felt dizzy then collapsed onto her bed.

"Should I call 911?" the health aide asked my mother.

"No," my mother responded. "Not now." She waited a few minutes more for my mother to improve before asking again.

"No," my mother responded again.

Defying my mother, she then called 911. By the time the paramedics arrived, it was too late, she told us.

My brother had the courage to look at my mother's body, but I did not.

"She's shorter," he remarked, looking rattled.

The police then confirmed that this would be the case: that we shrink upon death. We spent the next several hours with the policemen as we arranged for our mother's body to be taken to a synagogue. If we did not make these arrangements, the police would be required to call for the Los Angeles Coroner to take our mother to the morgue.

"You want to avoid that if you can," the presiding officer explained. "It can take up to two days to get her back once the county has her."

Our cousin Lauren suggested that my brother call the Sinai Temple. We waited for their arrival for more than two hours that afternoon, seated at our mother's white pedestal table with the officers, who filled us in on the particulars of their jobs: the thrill of high speed car chases, the role of the Sheriff's Department in physically subduing purportedly difficult detainees, and more. I appreciated the distraction the affable police officers provided us that afternoon, suspended as we were in the airy Park La Brea tower above the swaying date palms and loud water fountain below, suspended from the disturbing truth of my mother's lifeless body and what I felt at the time was my failure in helping her transition with dignity from this life to Emily Brontë's "endless and shadowless hereafter."

In the weeks, perhaps months, that precipitated my mother's death I woke each morning with the idea of ending my life. Before opening my eyes to another sunny day, I would imagine taking a razor blade to the veins in my arm in an effort to dull the pain and to put an end to it all. I felt hopeless in my certainty that my mother would never recover and, convinced we did not have the funds to care for her properly, feared her commitment to an underfunded state psychiatric facility when her money ran out. I couldn't imagine that in California public housing would be an option—in 2012, the state almost went bankrupt. No reassurance from my brother that my mother was improving countered these thoughts. Shortly before she died, perhaps a few weeks before, I dreamt that she was manic and viciously attacking me as she did when I was a teenage girl. Only in my dream, she was even more violent, stabbing me in the back multiple times with a large knife.

After my mother died, I no longer woke up compelled to slit my wrists. It was an immediate release. Despite this relief, I ached daily for her presence. At home I was numbed to the loss of my mother, yet grief-stricken almost from the moment I started up the car and left the Via Zurita. Subsumed as I passed through the familiar streets of Silver Lake, even more daunting was time I later spent meandering the aisles of grocery stores: Gelson's, Ralphs, Trader Joe's. All places I frequented trying to manufacture some sort of sustenance for my mother. Whenever my cell phone rang I wished it were her, noting the irony: that after years of averting her phone calls, her bold attempt to stay connected to the world outside the narrow confines of her illness, I would give anything to hear her voice on the other end of the phone one last time. Most of all, I felt deeply troubled that the last time I saw her I had fought needlessly with her, unsympathetic to her condition, one she had no control over and had struggled valiantly to live with for over forty years, perhaps more.

Mount Sinai, Simi Valley

My brother's speech at my mother's outdoor funeral was arresting. Wearing a yarmulke and fully composed, he spoke of her many accomplishments. Some, such as her pro bono work on amnesty, had been unknown to me at the time. He acknowledged the fact that he had lost his greatest "advocate."

"For better or worse," he said, "my mother called me every day, several times from the time I was sixteen years old. I still have over one hundred messages on my phone I have yet to erase."

And just as gracious was my great-aunt Freda, my mother's eighty-eight-year-old paternal aunt from South Africa. With a fractured rib and a painful hip, she was unable to walk the distance to the grave from the parking lot, so her daughter read the eulogy. Instead of being hidden from view, my mother was present among her family and recognized.

That our cousins took time from work to be there with us, and *for* her, was especially powerful, considering how difficult I found it to carve time out from my own fraught schedule. Watching my mother's coffin, a simple oak box adorned with a bouquet of long-stem flowers, angled into the deep rectangular groove cut into the ground, hawks flying overhead, golden canyon rock hailing in the distance, I understood for the first time the necessity of burying one's dead. Despite the stunning distance of this auxiliary mortuary from Los Angeles, roughly thirty miles, I felt some peace in burying my mother here. Initially having insisted upon cremation, I could not imagine the same relief in having her returned to me as ashes in an urn.

On grieving

The days that followed were as bad as people had warned.

"Losing a parent is one of the hardest things you will endure," a friend had often declared.

A cousin called to tell me about having lost her father, a man she was not on particularly good terms with at the time of his death, and that I would be haunted by the finality of my mother's passing.

"You will want to speak to them again, but you will not be able to." This would be an agonizing, estranging time.

After an initial day-and-a-half bout of maudlin weeping, I told myself that I had purged myself of the sorrow. In the coming days, my grief would lessen. After all, I had been mourning my mother's various losses for decades—her career, husband, suburban home, comportment, and mental health. I had shed my fair share of tears. I would soon be free of this long grieving process. I thought. Of course, that was simply fantasy. Meanwhile, my brother, systematic in his approach to life's challenges, researched grieving online, informing me of its demands.

"It should take about three months for the heavy grieving

to end. If it takes longer," he warned, "we should get some professional help." Unsurprisingly, this was the approximate time it took to stop weeping whenever I got into the car or shopped a supermarket aisle: places or activities that had become synonymous with caring for my mother.

After this time, even the distinctive sound of her voice began to fade. A predicament I came to rue almost immediately.

NMS

A week after she passed away, at dinner with a friend who works in the mental health field, I divulged the strange and difficult trajectory of my mother's final weeks. I confided my failing to acknowledge the symptoms of my mother's final illness. I just didn't understand why she continued to suffer from such extreme diarrhea. My mother had never suffered from an illness of this kind before, and I had been so slow to respond and felt ashamed.

"Yes," she explained her take. "It's fairly common for people who take antipsychotics to develop these sort of symptoms, a side effect of the medication."

Again, I was struck by the extent of my ignorance. Why hadn't I educated myself about the side effects of her medication? Why hadn't her doctors mentioned this possibility? This resonated with what I had read in biologist Ronald Chase's memoir, when he describes his brother Jim's final days—an inexplicable and rapid decline in which his organs began to fail him—and begins to consider that his brother's demise may have been an effect of his medications.

Chase remarks of his research into this topic, "I immersed myself in the psychiatric literature where I read about a condition known as neuroleptic (antipsychotic medication) malignant syndrome (NMS), described as 'an idiosyncratic, life-threatening complication of treatment with antipsychotic drugs that is characterized by fever, severe muscle rigidity, and autonomic and mental status changes.'" Elaborating further, he cites an *American Journal of Psychiatry* article, "The exact causes of NMS are variable, but 'nearly all case (studies) of NMS patients have reported physical exhaustion and dehydration prior to the onset of NMS. Elevated environmental temperature has been proposed as a contributing factor in some studies.'"[27]

It was extremely hot when my mother died. She was suffering from constant dehydration. Her lips were routinely peeling, chapped almost beyond recognition. Delusions were certainly a factor. Had she begun to suffer from a case of NMS? Could I have been better prepared for this end, or helped her better, if I had known what to expect?

---

27 Chase. 165–166.

As it turned out, my mother had died during the week of
Rosh Hashanah. Not a practicing Jew, I had little idea of its
significance beyond being the start of the Jewish New Year.
At a family celebration, another family member related by
marriage informed me that it was the only holiday in the
Jewish tradition in which we celebrated death. All other
celebrations focused on some element of life. I was stunned.
And I felt some relief. Romantically, just as I imagined
the spirit of departed F. Scott Fitzgerald mediating Zelda
Fitzgerald's death, when a fire erupted in a psychiatric
facility where she was receiving insulin treatments and
whose escape along with the other patients was "hampered
by locked doors, and heavy windows shackled with chains,"
I conjured a similar scenario in which during this Rosh
Hashanah week, my devoutly religious grandfather came for
my mother to usher her out of life. It was her time; he had
organized for this to happen. That her passage was not the
lonely one it most undoubtedly was.

Later, my brother confided in me a dream he had of finding
himself in the house we grew up in together, our mother in her
bedroom, in bed, confused and unsure of her predicament.

"You are no longer alive," he told her. "You can leave this place
now." He kissed her on the forehead, told her how desperately
we missed her, and the dream faded. In her troubled state,
I could only imagine the confusion that beset her as death
loomed in her periphery.

Shortly after the funeral, my mother's sister Anne called. We had hardly spoken over the years. As a young girl, I adored my aunt but rarely found myself in her company. On this occasion, she told me what it was like to be a woman in the 1970s living in Texas. How impossible it was for her to do the most ordinary things that I take for granted, without the approval of a husband. How she could not purchase a car without the permission of her husband. Or how she was unable to open up a line of credit at a department store, despite the fact that she owned a car and was gainfully employed. She fought handily with these corporate and bigoted foes. Marveling at my aunt's feminist prowess and impressed by the battles fought by an earlier generation of women, the conversation then turned to my mother's first breakdown in college. It was a story that I had not heard in detail before.

"Your mother used to call me in boarding school while she was studying at Oxford, and she would tell me stories of how the police were following her, or how they were watching her in the courtyard at St. Anne's, where she was a resident."

I imagined my twenty-year-old mother peering through sheer curtains of one of the red brick student housing blocks, frightened by these inexplicable hallucinations. "She would call to complain about strange smells and insist that she was dirty," Anne divulged. "I didn't know what to think."

The parallels were undeniable. During the past nine months, I had not confided in my aunt about the hallmark features of my mother's illness. We had hardly spoken during this time. Listening to my aunt's recollections, I came to realize that my mother's illness had taken the same shape her entire life.

The exceptional schizophrenic

As I grieved the loss of my mother, I continued to write on her illness. Of all the reading I did on the subject, Elyn Saks's bestselling memoir *The Center Cannot Hold*, a work I had once consciously avoided in an effort to distance myself from what I deemed a story of the "exceptional schizophrenic," was the hardest to endure.

Saks's story mirrored my mother's in two specific ways: first, she attended law school at Oxford, roughly seventeen years after my mother had. And it was there, just as it had been with my mother when she was on a fashionable fad diet, that Saks had her first full-blown experience of psychosis. From her, I discovered how inhumanely those with an illness might be treated. Being strapped down was a common early experience for Saks. During one internment by the EMT, she was actually placed under a net. The admitting doctor promised that they would not use restraints, but instead, once her trust had been earned, she was fastened with leather straps to the bed.

> I screamed at the top of my lungs and struggled against the group of hands pinning me down.... Then it got worse, since apparently binding my arms and legs wasn't enough. They arranged a net over me—an actual *net*—from the top at my neck to the bottom at my ankles, covering my legs, my torso, my chest. And then they pulled it snug at the four corners. I couldn't move at all, and felt like all of the breath was leaving my body.[28]

---

28 Saks, Elyn R. *The Center Cannot Hold: My Journey through Madness.* New York: Hachette, 2015. 149.

This experience of being admitted to the "seclusion room" of the Yale Psychiatric Institute terrified Saks, and in turn it terrified me. The jarring experience prompted her to research the use of restraints in America, discovering that at one time *over a hundred people a year died through their use.* I had to ask myself: Was this why my mother refused treatment? Had she been humiliated and hurt this way years before when she first became ill? Did she suspect that nothing could be done for her and that she might be brutalized before being forced to endure more powerful and ineffective electroshock therapy? Is this why she took such pains to hide her afflictions from outsiders? Why she muted herself in public and launched into frightening paranoid diatribes at home?

I had never considered my mother's plight from this perspective. I had never stopped to imagine what it might be like to confront such a limited set of options, what it might be like to know that an illness might place me in harm's way. Saks's powerful battle to sidestep the ravages of a drug treatment made only just available when my mother had her first break, through the reliance on the benefits of talk therapy alone, could not stop the disease's advance. When confronted by her doctor with the need to begin neuroleptic treatment, Saks recalls, "I knew exactly what a neuroleptic was—antipsychotic medication with terrible side effects, like heavy sedation, arms or legs that won't stop trembling (sometimes irreversibly), and a worst-case scenario that included death."[29]

29 Ibid.

Self-remonstrating voices

Like my mother, Saks was ambitious, tough. She had earned her ride at Oxford and was determined to make something of herself. Only after several bouts of the illness, dramatic episodes that nearly upended her budding career, did Saks relent and go the chemical route. As she tells it, a combination of anti-psychotics, Kleinian talk therapy, and deep committed friendships with men was what saw her through. Saks did not suffer from paranoia like my mother; she did not accuse others of conspiring against her although she was clearly burdened by powerful hallucinations and delusions. Instead, it appears her delusions were based on evil acts she believed she had committed herself. More often than not, she seemed to turn on herself and not on those she loved. In precise detail, she imparts the inner haranguing, the vicious taunts that assailed her as she went about her daily business:

> *Now she's walking down the street. She's ugly. People*
> *are looking at her. People are not to be trusted. People*
> *are looking at her. People are not to be trusted. Be*
> *careful. Be vigilant. They will hurt you. That*
> *man's face just turned into a monster's face. Be*
> *inconspicuous. Don't let them see you.*[30]

Did my mother battle with similar self-remonstrating voices? Was that why she insisted, whenever she relapsed, that she would not be welcomed wherever we went? My mother was not so fortunate as to find talk therapy at a young age or to make deep committed friendships with

---

30 Ibid. 76.

like-minded peers, although she had the ballast of my father's commitment to her and their marriage to keep her safe, until their divorce. Saks would go on to obtain a full professorship in law at USC and succeed in her profession as a mental health lawyer as well as marry. My mother would not be so fortunate as to earn a position in the working world beyond the self-employment that was bolstered in part by my father's stable salary. Had she been born a decade later or been encouraged to seek proper treatment sooner, maybe things could have been different.

My father's story

While Saks's parents apparently failed her, almost entirely distancing themselves from their daughter's life, her wedding, and other important celebrations, they had perhaps little access then to information on mental disorders to help them bridge the gap. My mother's father, a world-class doctor who confronted stigmatizing, brutal illnesses on a daily basis would seem to be in a different category altogether. That Grandpa Mike had hardly intervened on her behalf, securing or demanding that she get medical attention, was nothing short of ironic. My father seemed equally cognizant of this. One night at a family dinner in Pasadena, years before my mother would move to the West Coast, I asked my father what he thought of Grandpa Mike's lack of involvement. In Zimbabwe, I had heard multiple stories of his ability to diagnose impossible illnesses by more than one of his former patients. Why was he not able to do the same in my mother's case?

"Why didn't he do more for her?" I asked my father at dinner one night. "He was such an esteemed doctor."

"That's life's cruel irony," my father remarked sharply. "It's always much easier to solve other people's problems than it is to solve your own."

He then shared with me his experience of being engaged to my mother when she had a psychotic break in university during final exams. "Your grandfather lied to me," he recounted bitterly. "He told me that your mother would never get sick again."

At the time, my father was twenty-two years old and my mother was twenty. Whether my grandfather lied or not is not entirely knowable. It is possible he believed my mother's breakdown was caused solely by environmental factors, dieting, and exams. He would have clearly wanted for his striking, hard-working daughter a full, prosperous life. For how long he operated under this misconception, I cannot say. What information on mental disorders did he or my father have to help bridge the gap?

My mother maintained an unaffected mien for several years after marrying my father and bearing two children. Only when she began to work did her troubles magnify. It could be argued that had she not gone back to work, she may have never endured another psychotic episode. The genetic component of her illness may never have been triggered. But I find this view less than helpful. Who among us can steer clear of stressful challenges for an entire lifetime? Who would want to?

From my father's tone that evening, I took it that he felt robbed of his right to a happy family life, or perhaps more aptly, of making an informed decision.

Some distance

Almost a year to the day after my mother's death, after
years of working to keep "my salary up" and qualify for the
high-priced mortgage, I managed to purchase an eight-
hundred-square-foot house in the foothills of the San
Gabriel Mountains, in Altadena, a suburb of Pasadena
that had once been almost exclusively African-American.
The 1920s bungalow that I found, painted in the manner
of Colonial houses on the East Coast, a bright yellow with
long black shutters, made me think back on my childhood
in New Jersey. Mature deodar trees, sweet smelling Tibetan
firs, over one hundred years old, grace the front yard of the
house, and in the back of the unexpectedly large lot, is an
unobstructed view of the mountains. My mother would have
loved the place; she would have prized the trees and the
large parcel of land. I had her to thank for this. Her frugality
over the years had afforded me that last bit of help that I
needed.

Unpacking, I discovered an image of my mother that I
had never examined before—a tiny, black-and-white photograph with a thin white border. A girl of eight or nine is
sitting in her parents's garden on an unusually large woven
stool, her thin legs crossed at the ankles. Mom's hair is
parted on the side and worn in one large braid. Her forehead
is free of hair and her brows straight and neat. She wears a
schoolgirl dress in a chevron pattern with a Peter Pan collar.
Hands clasped carefully in her lap, she wears a slight smile.
Her eyes are steady and piercing. For what feels like the first
time, I see my mother, a bright-looking girl, poised dutifully
and without perceptible fear. Eyes trained on the boundless
years ahead.

Photo: Mara Feder

Acknowledgments

Thank you to all those whose encouragement and support of this book sustained me over the five long years it took to complete this memoir, particularly Orli Low, Susie McDonnell, Krystina Mierins, Linda Landels, Carrie Paterson, Allen Peacock, Rachel Mirriam Rehwald, Anna Joy Springer, and Irene Tsatsos.

I am also indebted to *Black Clock* magazine, helmed by acclaimed author Steve Erickson and Senior Editor Bruce Bauman, for commissioning an early work that is the basis of this book.

Thank you also to the staff and faculty of Critical Studies at CalArts for their influence and community. The institutional support of CalArts, SCI-Arc, UC Irvine, and Glendale College, where I have served for over ten years as Director of the Los Angeles Writers Reading Series, has sustained me in profound ways.

I am no less thankful to friends and family, many of whom are mentioned in these pages. A special thank you to my dear friend Alida Hanson for her generous and early support of this work, and much gratitude to Nike Schroeder for her keen eye and gorgeous cover design.

So much of my thinking has emerged from conversations with my guiding light, Connie Samaras, whose support and keen insight has been an essential part of the writing process.

Claire Phillips is the author of the novella *Black Market Babies* and recipient of the American Academy of Poets, First Prize. Her writing has appeared in *Black Clock* magazine, the *Los Angeles Review of Books*, and *Motherboard-Vice* among other places. She was nominated for the Pushcart Prize and received notable mention in *The Best American Essays 2015*. She teaches writing at CalArts, the Southern California Institute for Architecture (SCI-Arc), University of California, Irvine, and is Director of the Los Angeles Writers Reading Series at Glendale College. She holds a M.A. in Creative Writing from New York University, and a B.A. in English from San Francisco State University.